Berkshire
Edited by Tim Sharp

First published in Great Britain in 2007 by:
Young Writers
Remus House
Coltsfoot Drive
Peterborough
PE2 9JX
Telephone: 01733 890066
Website: www.youngwriters.co.uk

All Rights Reserved

© *Copyright Contributors 2007*

SB ISBN 978-1 84602 826 7

Foreword

This year, the Young Writers' *2007: A Poetry Odyssey* competition proudly presents a showcase of the best poetic talent selected from thousands of up-and-coming writers nationwide.

Young Writers was established in 1991 to promote the reading and writing of poetry within schools and to the young of today. Our books nurture and inspire confidence in the ability of young writers and provide a snapshot of poems written in schools and at home by budding poets of the future.

The thought, effort, imagination and hard work put into each poem impressed us all and the task of selecting poems was a difficult but nevertheless enjoyable experience.

We hope you are as pleased as we are with the final selection and that you and your family continue to be entertained with *2007: A Poetry Odyssey Berkshire* for many years to come.

Contents

Bearwood College
Alice Kennedy (13)	1
Mike Hutchings (13)	1
Sam Wright (13)	2
Vassilissa Conway (12)	3
Alice Probert (12)	4
Jennifer Bullers (12)	4
James Bailey (13)	5
Matthew Malins (12)	5
Chloe Taylor (12)	6
Lewis Gallagher (13)	6
James Dale (12)	7
James De Souza (13)	7
Emma Jane Moon (12)	8
Liam Read (13)	8
Marisa Rodriguez (13)	9
Amelia Wright (12)	10
Danni Macrae (14)	11
Karl Cochrane (13)	12
Eddie Gower (13)	12
Michael Jeffs (12)	13
James Solomons (12)	13
Bruce Locke (12)	14
Charlotte Moore (14)	14
Kier De'Ath (14)	15
Heinrich Koorts (13)	15
Matthew Dunn (14)	16
James Adams (14)	17
Natalie Wetenhall (15)	18
Emily Jeffs (14)	19
Edward Cole (14)	20
Kyle Absolom (14)	21

Highdown School
Bryony Davies-MacLeod (11)	22
Aimee Bowden (11)	23
Jessica Brooks (11)	24
Beth Leary (11)	25
Charlotte Ely (11)	26

Demelza Brooks (11) — 27
Richard Barrett (11) — 28
Alex Beaumont (11) — 29
Ellie Burrows (11) — 30
Rowan David Ilsley (11) — 31
Robert Brooks (11) — 32
Sarah Phillips (11) — 33
Emma Bingham (11) — 34

Ryeish Green School
Jasmine Collings (11) — 34
Victoria Jolliffe (11) — 35
Vicky Mercer (15) — 35
Jade Cocking (15) — 36
Anthony Rollason (12) — 36
Naomi Simpson & Elise Jones (15) — 37

St Bartholomew's School, Newbury
Eleanor Raymond (14) — 37
Ronan Hatfull (15) — 38
William Lockyear (15) — 38
Amy Leaver (14) — 39
Josh Whorriskey (14) — 39
Olivia Ward (15) — 40
Katie Curtis (14) — 41
Ellen MacIver (15) — 42
Joseph Minchin (14) — 42
Lauren Brown (15) — 43
James Brownell (12) — 43
Nikoo Atraki (15) — 44
Ben Sutcliffe (14) — 44
Alice Walker (14) — 45
Julian Hall (14) — 46
Rhonwen Lally (14) — 47
Thomas Crooks Smith (16) — 48
Georgia Jones (12) — 49
Sean Hart (12) — 49
Megan Newman (12) — 50

St Gabriel's School, Newbury
Natalie Hewitt (12)	51
Georgina Kreysa (11)	52
Nadia McAllan (11)	52
Hattie Wheeler (11)	53
Charlotte Brind (11)	53
Emily Bown (12)	54
Adrienne Hardwick (13)	54
Felicity Dodsley (12)	55
Joanne Atkins (11)	56
Grace Lake (12)	56
Emily Cammish (11)	57
Evie Harbury (12)	57
Rhia Honey (11)	58
Imogen Rolfe (12)	59
Claire Wood (11)	60
Alina Whitford (12)	61
Isabel Rudgley (11)	62
Georgetta Evans (12)	62
Georgia Hatton-Brown (13)	63
Charlotte Osborne (12)	63
Becky Weeks (12)	64
Danielle Johnson (12)	64
Sophie Fowler (12)	65
Bianca Rodriguez (12)	65
Charlotte Phelps (12)	66
Jessica Townend (12)	66
Georgia Robertson (12)	67
Melanie Davies (12)	67
Hannah Sutton (13)	68
Sarah Warwick (11)	68
Eleanor Baxter (12)	69
Emily Westcar (11)	69
Katherine Emo (12)	70
Holly Hall (11)	70
Lucy Wildsmith (11)	71
Beth Nichol (11)	72
Fiona Muir (12)	72
Miranda Porter (12)	73
Chloe Veal (11)	74
Larissa Hawkins (11)	75

Alice Martin (11) — 76
Antonia Wong (11) — 76
Chloe Watson-Smith (11) — 77
Maddy Rowley (11) — 77
Amy Hopes (11) — 78
Georgie Byfield (11) — 78
Rebecca Whittaker (11) — 79
Daisy Morley (11) — 79
Lily Rolfe (11) — 80
Olivia Shotliff (11) — 81
Joanna Ash (13) — 82
Charity Rankin (12) — 82
Leila Zarazel (12) — 83
Kimberly Ann Corrios Maravillas (13) — 83
Harriet Carver (11) — 84
Stephanie Snelling (11) — 84
Ella Nicklin (11) — 85
Emma James-Crook (13) — 85
Hannah Miles (12) — 86
Lucy Blanchard (13) — 86
Annabel Hawkesworth (13) — 87
Emily Anderson (12) — 88
Luisa Boheimer (13) — 89
Natasha Hookings (12) — 90
Elizabeth Hughes (12) — 91

The Castle School
Katie Thorne (13) — 91
Scott Yeates (11) — 91
Faye Douglas (12) — 92
Haddon Macdonald (12) — 92
Simon Ball (11) — 92

The Clere School
Monty Morgan (12) — 93
Alex Brown (12) — 93
Hannah Best (11) — 94
Sophie Elgar (11) — 94
Jamie Miles (12) — 94
Fern Dabill (12) — 95
Alexandra McGlone (12) — 95

James Bowman (11)	96
Jack Andrews (12)	96
Meghan Capewell (11)	97
Samantha North (12)	97
George Dyer (11)	98
Corinne Taylor (12)	98
Sam Price (11)	99
Tara Lewis (13)	99
Matthew Lawrence (11)	100
Ben Rampton (12)	100
Katie Scott (11)	101
Susan Connor (11)	101
Joshua Adamson (11)	102
Luke Otton (12)	102
Jaimie Schenkelaars (11)	103
Laura Skinner (11)	103
Sam Ingrorsen (11)	104
Emma Sygrove-Savill (12)	105
Cloé Higgs (11)	106
Chris Prozzo (12)	106
Kimberley Hutton (12)	107
Bethany Lawrence (12)	107
Jess Walford (12)	108
Sean Hills (12)	109
Jack Hibberd (13)	110
Gareth Wardhaugh (12)	110
Edward Rawlings (12)	111
Emily Gatehouse (12)	111
Nathan Prince (13)	112
Chris Clements (13)	112
Paige Prior (11)	113
Ryan Bardoe (12)	113
Hannah Read (12)	114
Nathan Cheshire (12)	114
Meg Hatton (13)	115
Bradley Smith (13)	115
Victoria Mackenzie (13)	116
Josh Sealey (12)	116
Joe Woodward (13)	117
Leo Minter (13)	117
Bryony Brichard (13)	118
Daniel Turner (12)	119

Nikki Slater (13)	120
Charlotte Osborne (13)	121
Melissa Goodwin (13)	122
Hayleigh Passfield (14)	122
Amy McMillan (13)	123
Claire Paterson (13)	123
Simone Such (14)	124
Abi Golding (13)	124
Claire Purser (13)	125
JJ Paine (14)	125
Lara Eaton (13)	126
Fran Duggan (13)	126
Jenny Harris (13)	127
Hannah Jones (13)	127
Charlotte Jones (13)	128
Claire Pasternakiewicz (14)	129

The Garth Hill School
Chelsea Johnson (15)	130

The Willink School
Carrie Taylor (14)	131
Rebecca Hill (14)	132
Rebecca Howarth (13)	133
Gareth Scott (13)	133
Rachel Winter (14)	134

The Poems

Love

Have you ever met someone
And they're so perfect for you?
Each day you fall deeper
In love with them
And you can't help it
And then a day comes
When you can't fall in love
With them anymore, it can be
The best feeling in the world
But all that can be shattered
Like when that person
Has that feeling for someone else
Especially if that someone else
Is a friend or even worse, a best friend
Then your whole world crashes around you
Because there is nothing that can
Hurt you as much as watching
The one you love
Love someone else
So remember when you break
Someone's heart, they have feelings
Just as you did with that one person
Who never loved you back.

Alice Kennedy (13)
Bearwood College

Pairs/Pears

Pairs are couples, pears are tasty
Everyone should never get hasty
All ravishingly delicious, enjoy them while they last
Really succulently, scrumptious, they're going fast.

Mike Hutchings (13)
Bearwood College

The Gypsy's Tale

A man had been a gypsy for all his life,
Travelling to and fro,
But there is a story of the gypsy,
That I think you should know.

As a young boy he was bullied,
As he did not go to school,
He was mocked by all in the town
And he was made to look a fool.

But the gypsy boy ignored them
And simply took it on the chin,
But if a person dare touch him,
He would throw them into the bin.

The gypsy boy was a big lad,
He knew it himself did he,
From all the fatty junk food,
He had to eat for tea.

But now, as an old gypsy,
In the same caravan he grew up in,
The gypsy man has eaten little
And is now relatively thin.

This is the simple life of a gypsy
And many could find this a bore,
But as he tells his story to his grandchildren,
They look at him in awe.

And thus, I end my story,
But I leave you with this,
If all are kind to one another,
Our lives are sure to be bliss.

Sam Wright (13)
Bearwood College

Love

A tiny spark that soon ignites into a flame
A naked flame that one must hold onto, so it keeps burning
Kindle the fire so that it may flourish and flow;
One would want this to be infinite
Like the snow it can melt away,
Like the seasons, it will change,
But determination will kick in,
So that when you feel lonely and dark you'll always have a safety net.
Trivial calamities will pass you by
As well as limits as far as trust is concerned.
But the innocent glow of one's love is true,
Yet the wilting tree may bear a resemblance to the scene it plays.
The leaves will stir and arguments will break out,
But in the end it would be worthwhile.
Defender of one's faith, to stand up for what you believe in;
This is the feeling called Love.
And in the end, age will etch a mark on you
And paint a beautiful picture which you will marvel at
You'll think back to your day of youth and laughter,
For now you have found something to live for;
Something to fight for.
To laugh in the face of danger; to laugh in spite of yourself
The happy days that you will share will stick to your mind like honey.
But then, suddenly, it's vanished, leaving you with bitter resentment.
In the blink of an eye, it's gone,
Washed away like the currents
And all you're left with are memories;
The thought of knowing that life will go on;
And so will love.

Vassilissa Conway (12)
Bearwood College

Growing Up

Baby lies, baby smiles
Baby loves, baby trusts

Infant sits, infant crawls
Infant laughs, infant plays

Toddler waddles, toddler speaks
Toddler imagines, toddler tantrums

Child learns, child explores
Child makes new friends

Pre-teen dreams, pre-teen cares not
Pre-teen hates, pre-teen moans a lot

Teenager rages, teenager fights
Teenager rebels, teenager's sad

Young adult parties, young adult drinks
Young adult has fun, young adult stinks

Adult cares, adult settles
Adult loves, adult taxes

Pensioner rests, pensioner travels
Pensioner limps, pensioner dies.

Alice Probert (12)
Bearwood College

In It To Win It!

Targeting to stay calm and awake,
Rasping hard, blood thumping fast,
In it to win it, is all I think,
Absolutely no sound reaches my ears.
Thumping and pumping breathing runs,
Hard and hefty, red and resty,
Lifted high, could easily die,
On and around muffled cries.
Now I am finished, senses return,
Sound and sense, breath so tense.

Jennifer Bullers (12)
Bearwood College

The Orange Tree

I sit so comfortably in my parent's
Soft, sweet flesh. All at home in the
Tough outer skin, protecting me. Me, so tiny
With so many other orange balls around.

My parents fall to the hard, cold ground
Away from the comfort of being suspended
From the tree. I pop out of my mother's
Flesh and lay myself in that cold, harsh ground.

I myself grow to be as magnificent
As all the other majestic trees
With plenty of bright orange fruit on me.

I drop my fruits at the end of
The blowy autumn. My oranges grow
Too, as grand as I once was and
I die down into the tender, tough ground.

James Bailey (13)
Bearwood College

The Sea

Glistening, shining, gleaming and blue,
All the fish gliding through,
Through the blue depths which are so deep
And at the end of the day, oh, how silent the depths sleep.

At night, oh, how very silent but so frightening,
All the black shapes gliding along.
It is all calm under the sea in the depths, but at the surface,
The thunder passes but the damage has been done
By the horrible lightning
Silence again.

Matthew Malins (12)
Bearwood College

Dreams

Dreams can set us to flight
Soar us away into the night,
Look at stars shining bright,
May our dreams set us to flight.

Flying past the planets glowing
You can feel the magic flowing,
See over the sun, forever burning,
As I find myself twisting and turning.

Next, I'm swimming in a deep, blue sea,
Now I'm swinging on a huge oak tree
In a place where the birds fly free
And man can live peacefully,
Swimming, swimming in a deep, blue sea.

Now my dream is coming to an end
It's time to say goodbye my friend,
For all dreams sadly come to an end
Goodbye, goodbye, goodbye old . . .

Chloe Taylor (12)
Bearwood College

Autumn

The different coloured leaves,
The gentle smell of rotting fruit on trees,
The general freshness in the air,
The wind blowing through my hair,
Leaves falling to the ground,
Twisting, turning all around,
Dead leaves crunching under my feet,
Beneath them lies such soft peat.
The mist rises from the fields,
As if they all have separate shields.
The sun begins to sink,
Making colours of red, orange and pink.

Lewis Gallagher (13)
Bearwood College

Pollution

Leaves are blowing in a winter breeze,
Monkeys are cold, down to their knees,
People scrapping for a bowl of peas,
Water flowing by and by,
But not in Africa, where rivers run dry.
Jets are destroying the ozone layer,
Whilst in Africa, water is rare.
Cars and planes are not so good
For our environment, where Jesus stood.
We make too much pollution,
So we need a solution.
Rainforests are being cut down,
Killing beautiful creatures all around,
The ice caps are melting too rapidly,
Let's stop and let everyone live happily.

James Dale (12)
Bearwood College

The Cat

Curled up in front of the warm fire
Makes life for her anything but dire,
Finding comfort among the snug pillows,
Whilst the world bends and billows.
As the night falls the bright, green eyes become hard
And the comforting complexion becomes marred,
Like a vicious animal who has been barred.
As she goes hunting for the night
Little vermin recoil in fright.
She searches in the dark abyss
For something easily missed,
She suddenly soars above her prey
And kills it without dismay.

James De Souza (13)
Bearwood College

The Bonfire

Autumn was approaching
The flowers fall dead, I sit and cuddle
My teddy in bed
The fire burned out
Too cold to even shout!

I lay down in my bed
With a pillow on my head
Dream of sunshine, warmth and happiness
My hair's untidy, my room's a big mess
I look out the window, watch the rain drizzle
That's when I start to see the bonfire sizzle . . .

In the night's waking sky
Thousands of ashes way up high
Not a fume of fire to be seen
Think the rain enjoys being mean
Grip the smoke, it's thicker than dust
The winter's showers, coldness and musk.

Emma Jane Moon (12)
Bearwood College

The Warrior Knight

A sword in a scabbard ready for battle,
A knight in armour, shiny and grey,
A Lord, too rich, too much power, too greedy.

A defence ready to fight,
A roll of drums to give courage,
A battalion of footmen, spears at the ready,
A row of archers, arrows fluttering in the wind.

A castle, a homestead, a heart and loved one to protect,
A casualty, a death, a life no more,
A high price to pay for war, not peace.

Liam Read (13)
Bearwood College

Immortal

Love, hate,
Life, death,
Hello, I'm here,
Bleeding my pain away,
For you, my love, proof I still live,
My soul alive forever,
We'll never be together,
Your rose will fall from your hand,
One day soon, you'll find your soul wandering,
Where as I shall never feel that,
Why is it I was to fall for you?
Landing in your sea of roses,
Alone and banished for an eternity,
You can't help me now, the job is done,
Try to reach me, then every step you take,
You feet will bleed more and more from the rose's thorns,
I can never leave, it's too late,
Tears run down my face always,
Stinging the cuts the thorns leave on me,
Why did you push me into this place?
This place where I forever feel,
Heartache, betrayal,
Deceit, hopelessness,
You'll leave me soon, I know it,
But until then,
Just take my hand, hold me close,
Then I'll be with you,
The one I love the most.

Marisa Rodriguez (13)
Bearwood College

Autumn

I can see the coloured leaves
Green, purple, red, yellow,
Golden leaves,
Lying on the ground
And twisting down the wind.
Rustling, rotting leaves
Hitting people's legs as they walk by.
Trees blowing in the wind,
Rain pattering on the windows.
I can see the fog
And mist in the distance.
I can feel the cold,
Frost, ice, wind and rain.
I can see people dressing up warmer,
With hats, scarves and gloves.
Animals getting ready for their hibernation.
I can see the frost and ice on the roads
And people scraping ice
Off their cars before work in the mornings.
I can smell fumes from car exhaust pipes.
In the evenings, I can hear
And see gritter lorries
Putting salt on the roads.

Amelia Wright (12)
Bearwood College

Traveller

The night I left in pain,
I was stranded in the rain,
The coldness shivered down my spine,
My fingers bled as bright as wine.

The rain poured down on me,
As flooded as the sea,
But then a house all on its own,
I ran to it and thought, *I'm not alone!*

As scared as I was in this cold, wet night,
I stood in the doorway in the moonlight,
I felt my heart fill with gloom,
As I entered the dark and dusty room.

This house was haunted, I could tell,
The ghostly silence and dreadful smell,
A scary voice echoed around the room,
With no light, except the moon.

It was time to leave, so I walked away,
Another voice said that I would pay,
This was a stupid choice and I should learn,
I took one last glimpse and I'll never return.

Danni Macrae (14)
Bearwood College

Sands Of Time

Swallowing me into the sands of time
The sand falling all around me
Time goes forwards, backwards and stands still,
In this place

Time is ticking away
The clocks strike away at each passing hour
The clocks go *ding-dong* as the hour passes
The sand falls down the hourglasses

I'm sinking into time itself
Shall I remain here for all eternity?
Now I'm stuck here for an eternity
Leaving footprints in the sands of time

Time flows forwards
Time flows backwards
Time even stands still
But time always wisps away each second.

Karl Cochrane (13)
Bearwood College

The Summer's Day

It was a peaceful, summer morning, with the sun beaming down
There were trees growing with leaves springing to life
There was a slight breeze spraying through your hair
You could hear birds in the trees singing a peaceful tune
As the long day was passing
The sun was getting hotter and hotter by the minute.

As the sun was shining, the lake was glistening
You could see the fish hopping out of the water
You could see the fishermen relaxing in the sunlight
As they were fishing
You could see the light breeze rippling across the lake
As the day was closing in
You could see the peaceful sun setting on the horizon.

Eddie Gower (13)
Bearwood College

I Love To Play Rugby

I love to play rugby,
It's my favourite game,
My position is flanker,
But I like them all the same.

I like to run with the ball
And knock over the opposition,
Shoulder down and run like the wind,
That's the correct position.

In the scrum, it sometimes gets hectic,
When everyone is pushing hard,
With the big props binding,
Standing like lumps of lard.

The winger is running up the line,
Time is ticking, is he going to score a try?
Yes, yes! He's scored! He's scored!
Times run out, it's a tie!

Michael Jeffs (12)
Bearwood College

The War

I am the age of 12,
A girl in despair,
Something is happening,
The Germans are taking over the Earth.

They are bombing and shooting everything in sight,
My mother, my father, also my sister,
So I hopped on a boat and went to Israel,
Leaving them in ashes to burn, choke and die.

All I had to do, was leave them behind
But it wasn't as easy to pretend
That I was so blind
Now I will tell you the story, of which, I hate.

James Solomons (12)
Bearwood College

Daddy's Porsche

It's slick, silver shaped, shiny,
Slithery, snake-like body.

It's grunting, goring, groaning,
Grumbling, gorilla grills.

The ravenous roaring,
Wreaking, reptile engine.

It's blinding, bright, brilliant,
Boastful, bear-sized beams.

Then when it's zipping zooming,
Zebra-like alone.

Instantly you know it's there,
But then it's gone, you don't know where!

Bruce Locke (12)
Bearwood College

The Journey Of A Thousand Nightmares

The journey of a thousand nightmares
Begins when a dream ends,
Like when your heart is broken
By your dearest love, or friend.

The Devil is like a dagger
Breaking your every thought,
Like a kitten torn from its mother
When it has just been bought.

Angels are there to guide us
But not there to heal,
They've ignored my pain and anger
I'm beginning to believe it's real.

Charlotte Moore (14)
Bearwood College

Morning Poem

Beep, beep, as my alarm clock goes,
I slowly wake up and scratch my sore arm,
Then my mother creeps in and screams, 'Morning!'

She opens the curtains and the trees are screaming in anger,
The flowers being ripped out of the ground
And I think, *here goes another school day!*

Smash! as my glass of orange juice falls over,
Argh! as I scream in an annoyed voice,
I then slowly crawl into my classic rover,
This, of course, was not my choice.

The car slowly pops along at a gentle speed,
We see all the children, walking along like ants, purposefully,
When it rains in the morning, it feels as though it is crying for me!

Kier De'Ath (14)
Bearwood College

The Tree

As I sat still
I knew his name would be Bill.
The wind blew
I felt something shiver in my shoe.
As I bent down to look
The tree shook.
I also felt the air
Rushing through my hair.
The leaves came tumbling down
Like rain in a town.
What fascinated me about this tree
Was its size and the way it was facing me.

Heinrich Koorts (13)
Bearwood College

The Long Path To Nowhere

I walk and walk down this path
It's been going on so long, you must be having a laugh
Or maybe, I'm just going daft.

I thought I was nearly at the end
But as usual, it was just another bend
Should I go back? It will all depend.

But then I saw some light
To my great delight
But then it had to go out of sight.

I walk, then I run
But I still could not see the sun
Oh, I wish I had a bun.

But then I saw
Was it a door?
Yes, yes, it was a door!

When I got to the door
I opened the door
And took one step and fell to a place with no floor.

Matthew Dunn (14)
Bearwood College

The Journey

Today I fall, no way back:
The life of an outsider I live.
The Amazon of life I live to walk
Alone on a world of green.

The leaves fall like a dead fox
I was a monster to those so small.
My feet they tread on things so dead
I walk in the middle of Hell.

I cut the flowers one by one
To make my walking path clear.
I wanted to run, my fear set aside
As the sky cried with rage.

As I start to get tired and struggle around
The walk, the answer must be clear.
The end of the journey with a normal life
A boat to make sure I survive.

The food was there at journey's end
Helpless as piece by piece is eaten.
A fisherman doing what he knows best
Catching me from the depths below.

James Adams (14)
Bearwood College

Journey Of An Angel

Her name means angel
She lived as long as she could
Her Arabian eyes, green as the emerald on her neck
Told the truth and I revealed
Her smile's so lethal, like the eye of a tiger
Beautiful and willing, but deadly and keen.

She's travelled the world and seen her dream
She met the love of her life, just like in the movies
But time went on and death killed their scene.

The heavens have kept her close to my heart
I haven't ever forgotten her
And she hasn't forgotten me.

I've seen her first crush
We've played boy chase girl
We've failed exams together and then drank till we hurled.

I went to her sleepovers
And she was the world
We've had bad times, I must admit
Like the time she became popular and I didn't fit.

I've watched her mature, from toddler to teen
But she'll always be the girl I've loved and teased.

She may be far away
But not far from me
Never to be forgotten
Her soul's stuck with me . . .

RIP.

Natalie Wetenhall (15)
Bearwood College

My Plane Odyssey

Ushered onto the plane
Like a herd of cows
Pushing your way through
The screams and rows.

Sit yourself down
And get strapped in
But first chuck your luggage
In the overhead bin.

As the engines roared
Like a grizzly bear
The woman behind me
Was sick in my hair!

'Chicken or fish?'
Came a voice from ahead
But as it got closer
I wished I was dead!

As I looked out the window
Land was in sight
Thank God it's over
It's been a terrible flight.

The wheels screeched
And it's come to an end
This cattle class journey
Has driven me round the bend!

Emily Jeffs (14)
Bearwood College

The Trip To School

I get in the car on a cold winter's day,
The exhaust rises like a phantom, I say,
The engine roars,
We slam the doors,
We join the other cars like a school of fish,
We will be on time for school, I wish.

We screech to a halt at the traffic jam,
Eager to avoid the police cam,
The small heater warms my face,
I realise how lucky I am to be in this place,
The heavens open and it begins to rain,
I remember my rugby injury and feel the pain.

We get closer, down Bearwood Road,
My maths homework looks like a code,
The rhododendrons are mountains,
My stomach is bubbling like a fountain,
We arrive at the gates,
I smile in happiness when I see my mates . . .

Edward Cole (14)
Bearwood College

I Have A Dream

I have a dream,
That one day everyone,
Would just live at peace
And just have some fun.

I have a dream,
That people will be equal,
No one to judge one another
And just follow the sequel.

I have a dream,
That racism is no more
And everyone loved one another,
If only that was the law.

I have a dream,
To live my dream,
To explore the world,
I am very keen.

That's my dream!

Kyle Absolom (14)
Bearwood College

Wandering

I see the dog
He is with the man
Down long empty streets
Passing rotten, empty houses
On bumpy, empty roads

The empty roads
Look haunting in the night
But neither dog
Nor man
Are scared by the streets
Or the petrifying rotting houses

Along the cold, rough roads
Seeing lots of rough streets
The dog settled down in the houses
In the pitch-black night
The cold lost little dog
Awaits the man

Wandering is the young man
Looking in dark, creepy houses
On the dark, creepy roads
Down the dark, creepy streets
Searching all through the night
Until he finds his beloved dog

After searching five days
The dog and the man are back at their houses
On their own clean roads
No more searching at night
The dog
And the man
Are back on their streets.

Bryony Davies-MacLeod (11)
Highdown School

Love

At home sits the girl,
With no one to love,
All she has is a puppy,
She needs someone to hug,
She tries to put on a smile,
But inside she is crying.

Who does the girl love
And who loves the girl?
She wants to stop crying,
The puppy wants a hug,
What a sad, little puppy.

Why is she crying,
When she has a puppy?
He wants her to smile,
He needs her to love,
He asks the girl,
To give him a hug.

A man sees the puppy,
He loves the girl,
She is no longer crying,
She can now smile,
She has her hug,
She has her love.

Forever now she can smile,
Now that she has her love,
The man loves the girl,
He has stopped her from crying,
She can always have a hug,
Now she has a man and a puppy.

Aimee Bowden (11)
Highdown School

The Lioness

The lioness stops, waiting to pounce
As the sun sets on the horizon, glowing
Like a ruby. As she lies, sleek
And as she waits in the silent
Jungle, the noise of another lioness as she creeps
Towards the same antelope, the only noise, the padding of her paws.

As the she-lion jumps, her padded paws
Unleash the claws which were waiting for the pounce.
When she feels the flesh, a pair of eyes glowing
With rage turn to face the lioness who was so sleek.
A lion's roar breaks the silent
Atmosphere, while away the antelope creeps.

The fight is over in seconds; the injured creep
Away into the bushes; the triumphant lioness pounds
                              along the ground,
Her beautiful paws
Flying over the barren grass, savouring her pounce.
The dark sky is relit by the glowing
Moon, as the she-lion, so, so sleek
Continues the hunt, her territory silent.

Quickly, she rediscovers the antelope and silently, so silently
The graceful lioness begins to creep.
Her delicate, yet strong paws
Long to attack, to pounce
But the cunning side of her says no, the glowing
Waterhole surrounded by no animal as sleek

As herself and then she leaps, her body sleek
The waterhole is filled by panicking animals who were once so silent.
Many try to creep
Away unnoticed, but they are too slow for the she-lion's paws.
The lioness' pounce was worthwhile,
She thinks as she licks her lips, her eyes forever glowing.

Jessica Brooks (11)
Highdown School

Deep In The Jungle

Deep in the jungle,
There lay a tiger
Thawing out in the sun
But watching him while they are swinging
Is a bunch of mysterious monkeys

The swinging
Of the mysterious monkeys
Has put the colourful tiger
To lay in the hot, hot sun
The tiger died from lack of water, deep in the jungle

The tiger's brother roars in the jungle
At the mysterious monkeys
For putting his brother in a trance in the hot, hot sun
The monkeys see the darting stripes
And run from the tiger

The poor monkeys
Are running from the vicious tiger
Then gleaming in the sun,
The tiger gets the better of the monkeys . . .
There is a monkey, dead in the jungle

The vicious tiger
Is racing after the monkeys
It was all the swinging
That put his brother to die in the sun
There is going to be another kill in the jungle

There were more kills in the jungle
Now there are no more monkeys
No more swinging
Just a spirit of an angry tiger
Killed by the hot sun.

Beth Leary (11)
Highdown School

The Ocean

I see a dolphin
Jumping and swimming
In the glistening, deep water
Diving down to catch a school of fish
I watch the ocean
The ocean that is big, massive and blue

I see different shades of blue
All over the back of the dolphins
Far out in the ocean
Leaping and swimming
Searching for colourful fish
Down in the sparkling water

There are many mysteries in the ocean
Especially in the dark, murky water
Who knows what is swimming
Down in the dark blue?
Does the dolphin?
Do the fish?

Maybe some fish
Know what is in the ocean
But still the dolphin
Leaps through the water
Through the turquoise blue
He spends most of his life swimming

Many creatures must be swimming
Apart from the colourful fish
Down in the rippling water, so blue
There is history beneath the bed of the ocean
Lying silently and still under the water
So different from the dolphin.

Charlotte Ely (11)
Highdown School

In The Forest

I see the deer
Leaping swiftly in the forest
Feet silent on the ground
His coat shining in the morning sunlight
Surrounded by dark, tall, friendly-looking trees
Where everything is quiet

The soft, brown, forest ground
Gleaming in the golden sunlight
With shadows from the green emerald trees
Is the great, proud deer
Quite, content and so, so peaceful and quiet
In the amazing, glorious forest

I then see by the crystal-clear stream, is the drinking deer
His antlers tall with the shadow from the trees
And around him, is the dark, brown, wet ground
Though it is all very quiet
In the silent forest
Then I also see a robin singing sweetly, glowing brightly in the sunlight

Then suddenly, he's joined with other beautiful deer
And they too are quiet
As they sniff around the forest
They seem to enjoy the sunlight
And they love the soft, brown ground
But soon they make a move, running off among the trees

They're running all together in the sunlight
With the shadows of the trees
Jumping carefully in the forest
So they lived there forever in the morning sunlight
Surrounded by trees
In the beautiful forest.

Demelza Brooks (11)
Highdown School

The Race

Every single car
Is behind the starting line,
The Ferrari starts driving
While my Porsche is in the pit stop,
The engine starts roaring
I hope I don't crash.

The Mustang's had a crash,
Lost control of its driving,
Its engine stops roaring,
As it pulls into the pit stop
I've passed the checkpoint line,
I've got a very fast car.

The crowd begin roaring
As the Ferrari goes in the pit stop,
Ahead is the check point line
And many other cars,
Oh no! the Viper's stopped driving
I think I'm going to crash!

I skid into the pit stop
That was a severe crash
My engine no longer roaring
No hope of crossing that finishing line,
No hope of beating the other cars,
My car won't start driving.

Hooray! the engine is roaring,
I begin to start driving,
That kamikaze car
Is still in the pit stop,
From that suicidal crash,
Yes! I've won! I've passed the finished line.

Richard Barrett (11)
Highdown School

Bullying

I see the girl
Surrounded by the bullies
So patient, she is waiting
But still she is shaking
Wanting to fight
But is too petrified

Time is ticking on, waiting
Ever so patiently is the girl
Still constantly shaking
And still so very petrified
Of the bullies
And still too scared to fight

With courage the girl
Stands up and fights
Not waiting
And not petrified
No longer shaking
And not worried about the bullies

Now the bullies
Are petrified
Of the girl
And she is waiting
For them to start shaking
And not to fight

The girl
Got her way by waiting
And the courage to fight.

Alex Beaumont (11)
Highdown School

The Big Race

In the air I see my murky breath
Steadily quickening is the pace
Everyone else so fit, runs quicker through the course
How I plead to see the finish
My feet widen to make larger my step
Inside I know really how much I need this race

The girl next to me, steadies the pace
Much harder is my step
More and more thickening is the pace
All I see ahead, is the muddy, tired course
All more demanding is the race
I still see no finish

Bewildered and confused I lose my step
I feel friction under my feet, as I step off the course
Suddenly and very unexpectedly, I am off and out of the race
I am panting, hopelessly trying to catch my breath
No chance of that finish
I have lost the girl who set that pace

In the far distance, blurred and fuzzy, I see the finish
Was I really still able to take some more steps?
People still hopelessly trying, for the win of the race
I've caught my breath!
Slowly and steadily I get back to the course
Gradually I get back the pace

It's true, all I need now is a few more steps
Everyone still battling and playing, for the win of the race
No longer am I looking at the course!
No I am gazing at the finish
Like ice is my breath!
I am holding that pace!

Ellie Burrows (11)
Highdown School

In The Jungle

Everywhere is green,
In the vast jungle,
All the plants are swaying, swaying,
Everything is noisy,
Because of all the animals,
Trying to find cover from the rainstorm.

In the tropical depths of the jungle,
The plants are still swaying, swaying.
All of the colourful animals,
Are still hiding from the rainstorm,
They're still being extremely noisy,
Hiding in the green.

The plants have stopped swaying, swaying,
The animals have stopped being noisy,
But still trapped because of the rainstorm,
Raining on the jungle,
Where everything is green,
Scared are all the animals.

All the wet animals,
Are petrified of the rainstorm,
Pitter-patter, but it is still very noisy,
In the cold, wet jungle,
Which still shines bright, bright green,
I can't hear any swaying, swaying.

Everywhere is looking gloomy instead of green,
But it is still very noisy
And all the cold, wet animals
Are still hiding from the raging rainstorm,
But still there is no swaying, swaying.
In the mighty jungle.

Rowan David Ilsley (11)
Highdown School

The Child

In the closed school,
There is a ghost child,
Working beyond the grave, eternally bored,
Using an empty pen
His work book is on a non-existent desk,
He underlines with a broken ruler.

Then he drops the ruler,
The noiseless click reverberates around the silent school
He ducks beneath his desk
And the ruler is retrieved by the child
And once again he writes with his empty pen,
More and more bored.

Then he goes to the maths room, only slightly less bored,
He drops his ruler
And his pen,
Onto a hole on the floor of the school,
He retrieves the pen and ruler, then the child
Sits at a desk.

There is a hole, but he sits at the non-existent desk
And becomes incredibly bored,
The lonely child,
Can't find his ruler,
Working with no ruler in the empty school,
Using an empty pen.

Then the child changes his pen,
Also inkless, writing in his book, on the non-existent desk,
Within the ruined school,
Doing maths, he is bored,
Not needing his ruler,
On works the child.

Robert Brooks (11)
Highdown School

Rabbit

My white, fluffy rabbit
With golden, fluffy fur,
Hops around the garden,
Lit up by the burning sun
Hanging in the clear blue sky

My sweet, calm rabbit
With glistening fur,
Hops around the garden,
Blinded by the sun
Beaming down from the sky

There are many clouds in the sky
And far below sits a sweet, little rabbit
With long, delightful fur,
I watch as she pounces around the garden
And it dims as the cloud pile over the sun

As the clouds cover the sun,
Fill the sky,
I stroke my tired rabbit,
My hands run through her soft fur,
As the sun peeps out from the clouds

It is still dusky over the garden
As the clouds fight the sun
For space in the sky,
I say goodnight to my rabbit,
I brush the mud from her fur

Her white, soft, fluffy fur
Is in darkness with the garden
As the clouds have covered the sun
And have filled the sky
It's sleep, for my rabbit.

Sarah Phillips (11)
Highdown School

The Little Ballerina

Dull as death lay the studio,
It's heartbeat the teacher.
Broken down was the girl,
Who was to dance,
To become a ballerina,
On a stage far, far away.

Practise makes perfect, said the teacher,
If you want to become a ballerina.
Touched by her words, was the girl,
Who was to dance.
For now her fairytale had gone away,
There before her, was the studio.

No longer as weak and petrified was the girl,
Grabbing her pride before it went away.
She herself was a ballerina
And alone was the teacher,
In the lonely studio.

Now bright and shining was the studio,
The place where she left to run far away.
And left behind was her old teacher,
So she went onto dance to be
The little ballerina.

Emma Bingham (11)
Highdown School

Aeroplane

As I get on the plane, I feel happy inside.
As the captain states the rules, I beam.
As they say it's just about to take off, I can't wait.
As we fly over the countries I feel tired and then fall asleep.
When I wake up we are about to land, butterflies in my tummy.
Then when we get off, I feel the best I've ever felt.
Then I say, 'Great, we're in South Africa.'

Jasmine Collings (11)
Ryeish Green School

The Mirror

When you get what you want,
In a struggle for self,
And the world makes you king
For a day.
Just go to the mirror,
And look at the odyssey
In yourself,
And see what the man
Has to say.

The person whose judgement
Counts the most,
Is the person who is staring
Back in the glass;
But remember too,
Never put on a mask!

Victoria Jolliffe (11)
Ryeish Green School

Sanctuary

Mellow brown,
cold breeze, shifting through the window.
Past memories stare from the shelf,
the computer whispering softly.

The radio shrills to its hearts content,
pages flick and giggle in the breeze,
images of fantasy lie on the floor
telling the tales of a little girl's life and dreams.

This is my home.
This is my sanctuary.
The place a feel safe,
a place full of dreams,
a place where I can just be me.

Vicky Mercer (15)
Ryeish Green School

Family

Without my family, where would I be?
The comfort from your own mum and dad is clear to see
You know it's true, you know it's real with true love
Because the true things for me are sent from up above.

They're the people who brought you to life
Those nine months Mum put up with pain and strife
It just shows the true feelings they feel for you.
They give love, they suffer, they put things off for you too.

But being a child, you don't realise things
Things like money and time and sufferings
Things like this I take for granted
They're the ones who got my life started.

They take me everywhere I need to go
There's barely a time when they end up saying no.
Even if they had plans, they would cancel them for me,
The true love they give is there for me to see.

They always think I don't appreciate the things they do
But I love them a lot and would do anything for them too.
I know we'll have our ups and downs in the year throughout
But is that not what a family is all about.

Jade Cocking (15)
Ryeish Green School

The Big Day

I open my eyes and pull the curtains,
The sun is gleaming through the window at me,
Today is the day I've been waiting for,
Today is the journey day.
In the car, along fast roads,
Through towns, villages and past farms,
The scenery changing faster and faster.
I am there. The vast white horse of Westbury
Stands in front of me.
'Hello Nan and Ted!'

Anthony Rollason (12)
Ryeish Green School

Boogie Bones

It was a Friday evening
One week ago exact
That funky Friday feeling
All my boogie bones intact.

Everyone's a drunken mess,
The drinks are now half full.
Guys and dolls prepared to impress,
The party begins to dull.

The beer cans left empty
All scattered on the floor.
People tired from drinking plenty
Their boogie bones now sore.

Naomi Simpson & Elise Jones (15)
Ryeish Green School

Whose Point Of View?

Whose point of view is it, they ask
The protagonist's or his brother's?
But how do I know?
I can't even work out my own point of view.
If I don't even know how I feel,
How do I know how the character feels?
I don't even know what I'm going to do in the future
So how can I predict what the bad guy's plans are?
What type of camera shot is it? The question asks
Is it low-angle, mid-shot or does it pan across?
But how do I know, when I don't even know
What my own take on life is?

How can I know? Who does know? Does anyone?
Will they tell me? Will it help me decide on my future?

It might get me to the exam hall, to the question paper
To the short story and then the question -
Whose point of view is it?

Eleanor Raymond (14)
St Bartholomew's School, Newbury

Dear Frustrated Superstar

I am a frustrated superstar,
Every time I pick something up,
It seems to turn to gold,
But then it rusts away.
Why can't life be easy?
Why can't we make the transition,
Without going through the bends?
Life has no dead ends.

I'm so tired,
To think about so many things,
Don't want to sink to that level.
Just keep your head in the clouds,
Think what it would be like,
To be on cloud number nine.

Dear frustrated superstar.

Ronan Hatfull (15)
St Bartholomew's School, Newbury

The Soldiers

The soldiers are ready at break of the dawn,
Brought into line by the sound of a horn.
Gazing down from the top of the hill,
Like hawks they stare; yes, they're here for the kill.

Mortars are hailing, down from the sky,
The soldiers fight but they're here to die.
An Angel of Death in the Valley of Doom,
Spreading its wings like an opening tomb.

The soldiers have died, the hawks have gone,
The Valley of Death sings its woeful song.
So end the bloodshed and listen to me,
This is the darker side of humanity.

William Lockyear (15)
St Bartholomew's School, Newbury

My Identity

You ask about my identity
From the colour of my eyes, to how I see
And how I stand or my circle of friends
As you watch me try and follow the trend
All dressed up but nowhere to go
My story turns into a tale of woe
The high class status I had all around
Just suddenly comes crashing down
On the surface I'm all loud and brave
But deep down, it's me I want someone to save
Life is what you use and make
And all things in it you have to take
Your identity is full of things
Of what comes and goes or gives and brings
Your personality, image and how popular
Makes you who you really are
So there you go, now you see
That is my identity.

Amy Leaver (14)
St Bartholomew's School, Newbury

Dancing Dragons

Dancing dragons in the sky,
Fire beasts frolic up so high,
Beneath the peasants calmly wait,
For the giant gods, they love and hate.

Comets race past, celestial being,
Escaping danger without us seeing,
Below the common slowly live,
As life passes by like grain through a sieve.

Dancing dragons on the land,
Kings of water, earth and sand
Up above the peasants wait,
The fire beasts are fashionably late.

Josh Whorriskey (14)
St Bartholomew's School, Newbury

#2648

What has identity got to do with me?

My interests
My friends
My self-image
Me.

That is who I am to me
But my identity is who you suppose me to be
My place in the world is where you put me
Every move
Every breath
Every day
That I make, that I take,
Is my identity.

Because every move
Every breath
Every day
I make, that I take
Is how you judge me.

I am in the box you put me in,
I am holding hands with the prejudices you thought of me.

What has identity got to do with me?
Life is how you make it
Identity is how you fake it.

What is identity?
It is your judgements.

Olivia Ward (15)
St Bartholomew's School, Newbury

Broken Rock Star

Look, it's broken rock star,
I say to my mirror friend,
His skin is drawn,
He looks really worn,
Look, it's broken rock star.

Tell me, broken rock star,
What's happened to your voice?
His hoarse voice replied to me
My lungs have sung this song for too long
And it's true, I hurt too
Remember when they loved you.

Defenceless little rock star
He lost himself to the limelight,
He only wanted to play music,
To do things his way
To do things right.

Oh, poor, little broken rock star,
My mirror image sighs
Tears are brimming I can see
They are unshed and burning his empty eyes.

He never really imagined
He'd lose himself on the way
You're not yourself today Charlie,
You're a broken rock star,
Tomorrow, yesterday and today . . .

Katie Curtis (14)
St Bartholomew's School, Newbury

Identity

She wanders under the moonlight
With a vacant space,
Occupying her tears.
She cannot stop them falling;
Someone stole her identity, see.
Someone took the very heart she had wanted to protect.

He wanders under the sunlight
With a satisfied smile,
Occupying his thoughts.
He cannot stop remembering;
He stole her identity, see.
He took the very heart she had wanted to protect.

They had wandered under the starlight
Both had been smiling free,
Occupying their hearts.
They could not stop their feelings;
They both had identities, see.
They were both protected by the other's love.

But the protection left,
As did the love
And under the bleakest sky;
They lost their identities.

Ellen MacIver (15)
St Bartholomew's School, Newbury

Bovine Identity

The cellophane wrapping said he,
Was born in Scotland.
Did he know this?
It said he,
Worked well as a roast.
Did he imagine this?
Did the wrapper know more than he
About his personal bovine identity?

Joseph Minchin (14)
St Bartholomew's School, Newbury

Youth

Youth knows everything,
But in reality, it knows nothing.
What do I know?
I'd tell you,
If I could,
But I need to work it out first.
What do I know?
I'd tell you,
If I could,
But I need to see for myself.
What's in the world.
What do I know?
I'd tell you,
If I could,
But I'm creating my own morals,
My own beliefs.
Youth needs experience to learn,
I thought that to myself the other day
And realised
That's something I know.

Lauren Brown (15)
St Bartholomew's School, Newbury

My ID

My ID
It's who I am, it's me.

If you tell me
I may forget

If you show me
I may regret

I know you, you know me
That's the way it's going to be.

James Brownell (12)
St Bartholomew's School, Newbury

When The Lights Go Out

When the lights go out
Darkness descends
And once again, I comprehend
What's left of you? Of us? Of me?
The others, they cannot yet see.
For when it's light and day has come,
To me you're not the only one,
But at night, when moonlight falls,
It is your name I long to call.
And in this bed, I sit and gaze,
In once again, a lovestruck haze,
At this bed where you once lay
It's empty now, to my dismay.
And although, you've been long gone,
My dreams have now been over-shone
By sadness, fear, anguish and doubt,
I still reminisce when the lights go out.

Nikoo Atraki (15)
St Bartholomew's School, Newbury

Identity Theft

'Funny,' the police officer said
I can't believe that's your real trait
Maybe James is the name of a mate
However, it seems you're guilty of an identity take.

You say your real name is Daniel
But that doesn't match with my database
I strongly feel you've lied to me
The courts, the crown, my democracy.

Maybe a spell in gaol will change your ways
Stop you from stealing someone else's personality
Stop you taking their identity
And changing it - irresponsibly.

Ben Sutcliffe (14)
St Bartholomew's School, Newbury

Suicidal Story

Slowly tears fall down my face
People tell me that I'm a disgrace
I wish they'd stop hurting me
I'm trying to be good; can't they see?
Tears drip down to my pillow
As I stare at the willow
Tree outside my bedroom
Rain clouds reflect my inside gloom.
I sit at the desk at school
I feel like such a fool
Classmates snigger at me all around
Can't I be swallowed by a hole in the ground?
I just want my life to end
The teasing and bullies drive me round the bend
No matter what I do, it is never good enough
For anyone at all, but still I try to stay tough.
But it's no use, I'll still cry
Every single day, I cry
Everyone wants to make me cry
I'll save myself the hurt and I'll just die.
Jump off the bridge - do it, do it
I mustn't chicken out - got to go through with it
I promised and told myself that I'm strong
Bloody hell, I sure was wrong.
I'll do it now, oh yes I will
I'll jump off this bridge and be killed
People are watching me from the floor
Soon I'll join them, in all my gore
Or is it my glory? Gory glory
This is my life - a suicidal story.

Alice Walker (14)
St Bartholomew's School, Newbury

Searching In The Dark

A boy adrift
In a sea of emotion,
Trapped in a tempest
That lives in his heart.

Stranded, alone,
Searching for himself
Among others
Who are doing the same.

He cries out
In the night,
But he is alone
Inside himself.

'Who am I?' he asks
But nobody answers,
They can't,
They're asking themselves the same question.

Outside he is calm,
But inside he is running,
Sprinting, through the dark that surrounds him,
Searching for the light.

He demands answers,
He gets silence,
For he is alone,
Lost within himself.

Julian Hall (14)
St Bartholomew's School, Newbury

The Ocean

As the waves crash against the shore,
Rain hurtles down through the sky.
In a fury of uncontrolled anger,
The sky lets out a flash of lightning.

The pitch-black sky lights up,
Then the sound of thunder.
Ringing in your ears,
Dulling the senses.

The waves attack the rocks,
With an almighty smash of water.
Yet the rocks stand bravely,
Unaffected by the rage.

And still the ocean carries on,
In its reckless rage.
Throwing objects around,
Inconsiderate of the world.

But then comes the morning
And as the city starts to wake,
Daylight comes
And the sea calms.

Now all is still,
The night has been forgotten.
But only until sunset,
When the storm will come again.

Rhonwen Lally (14)
St Bartholomew's School, Newbury

Identity Mish-Mash

'A question?' says old man to friend
Sitting in a bar, sips drink.
'All these teenage fashions,
What do you think?'

'If I were to have a say,'
Says one man to the other,
'I would say that all these teens,
Look like one another.'

'Hmm,' says the first man, scratches beard.
He looks at teens sat up at bar
Both in pink with matching scarves,
'Look how good they think they are.'

'Do you think they even see?
Notice how she looks at me?'
'Aye, just like the other one,
Where's their own identity?'

Two young girls sit at a bar,
They turn to look at two old men
Tall girl says to shorter
'Aren't you so glad we're not them?'

'Oh, God yeah!' says shorter girl,
'They have no fashion sense at all
Why do all old men wear tweed?
Can't they be original?'

'Hmm' says first girl, sipping wine,
'And why is it always older men
That send a shiver down your spine
From staring at your chest?'

'I know babe! God, they're all so lame,
And what's worse, they're all the same.'
'I know darling, don't tell me,
They've lost their identity.'

Thomas Crooks Smith (16)
St Bartholomew's School, Newbury

Australian Girl

A n Aussie girl is who I am
U K is where I live
S nakes and spiders are my biggest fear
T welve is my age
R eliable, generous and a good friend are some of my qualities
A thletics isn't my thing
L ollies, pasta and chocolates are my favourite things to eat
I have blue eyes, blonde hair, I'm skinny and tall
A rt is one of my hobbies
N etball, swimming and dance are my hobbies too

G eorgia is my name
I have travelled halfway across the world
R emembering leaving friends makes me sad
L oyal, outgoing, enthusiastic and joyful
    are the words that describe me.

Georgia Jones (12)
St Bartholomew's School, Newbury

Identity

Identity, identity,
What is identity and what does it mean?
It's who you are and what you are
And everything about you
We're not the same
No one's the same
'Cause I am me
And you are you
For that is our own identity.

Sean Hart (12)
St Bartholomew's School, Newbury

A Poem About Me!

Hello, my name is Megan,
I hope to go to Heaven.
I am twelve, nearly thirteen,
I like to be treated like a queen.

I hope to get a good job
And marry a man called Bob.
I hope to get a car
And travel far.

I wish I could fly,
But in the process, I don't want to die.
I wish I had a talking dog,
That could see me through the fog.

I like pizza and chips,
When I have finished, I lick my lips.
I like shopping for shoes,
But when my friends don't come, I get the blues.

I don't like mushrooms, fish or eggs,
When I eat them, I get shivery legs.
I don't like moths,
So I cover them with cloths.

I am nice, kind and caring
And very good at sharing.
I am a good friend and polite,
I try to be cheerful and bright.

Megan Newman (12)
St Bartholomew's School, Newbury

New To St Gabriel's Senior School

In the morning,
About to cry,
Thinking,
God, let me die!

Mum
Says everything's going to be all right
But, she has to say that!

In the car,
So nervous, so scared,
Didn't want to leave home.

When I arrived,
I saw the faces of my friends,
Then I knew it wasn't just me!

In the classroom,
I felt, when is this day going to end?
It seems like never!

In the end,
It all turned out OK,
I had a brilliant day.

My mum was right:
I had nothing to fear,
In the end.

Natalie Hewitt (12)
St Gabriel's School, Newbury

My First Day In Senior School

I waited at the school gates,
My legs trembling with fear.
I waited for one of my friends to show me,
Where the classroom was,
When I was at the door.

People seemed to be really excited,
I supposed it was the first day,
They should be.

I was a tiny, tiny bit excited
Compared to how scared I was!
When everybody started to arrive
I felt quite a lot better.

The teachers introduced themselves
And took the register.
By now I was quite excited,
Lessons went by really fast,
Before I knew it,
It was the end of the day,
I had a great new day!

Georgina Kreysa (11)
St Gabriel's School, Newbury

New School

Nervously,
I walked
Into my new school.
I saw a sea of new faces.
Excitement bubbled through my skin.
I recognised a few people,
In amongst the crowd.
A new uniform and a new feeling:
It felt like a new country.

Nadia McAllan (11)
St Gabriel's School, Newbury

My New School

Walking up to the entrance,
Feeling scared and nervous.
Then I saw my friend
In the distance!
Waves of relief poured over me,
As I knew I was not alone
Any longer.

Walking into the square hall,
I felt as small as a mouse,
Everyone seemed so much bigger.
Reporting in to Mrs Sams,
Finding my classroom,
Was a relief.

The day ahead
Was very exciting:
Meeting new teachers,
Making new friends.

Hattie Wheeler (11)
St Gabriel's School, Newbury

Senior School

I sit in the car waiting,
Waiting for a friend to come
And lift me out of my drowning fright.

When I see others walking in, I see a door opening,
Opening at the end of the tunnel.
My fright clears,
I see my friend running towards me,
A sigh of relief, I'm not alone.

I climb, what seem, endless stairs
And then my classroom's there,
Pushing a door, my friends stand their smiling:
The term is beginning.

Charlotte Brind (11)
St Gabriel's School, Newbury

My New School

I was feeling nervous
As I came up the drive,
I was feeling worried and excited.
When I got into the classroom,
I was relieved to see my friend.

At the end of the day,
I felt like
I was going to drop!
All the lessons felt long.
I got onto the bus to go home
I felt relieved
I had no homework.
When I got off the bus at my stop,
The first thing my mum said was,
'How was your day?'

Emily Bown (12)
St Gabriel's School, Newbury

Hired Man

Left to die in a cold, dark room,
      A hired man.
I brought myself back,
      A hired man.
I tried to help my enemies,
      A hired man.
I was rejected,
      A hired man.
I was brought back by the men who left me to die,
      A hired man.
I worked for them,
      A hired man.
I was left to die in a cold, dark room
And this time I'm not coming back . . .
      Is that all I am?
           A hired man.

Adrienne Hardwick (13)
St Gabriel's School, Newbury

Senior School

I stood at the door, my new
Life about to start.
My hands started sweating,
My eyes were filling with
Tears.
Where was I going to go?

Then Miranda came
Charging,
'Here, come with me,' she
Said.
So relieved,
I'd found my new
Classroom.

Then everyone started
To arrive,
New people everywhere.
Then one girl arrived;
I've never seen her before!

I go over to see her,
My heart was pounding;
What was I going to say?

Then she smiled
As I spoke to her!
She looked so happy
And that made me feel good
Too.

End of the day,
I'm so relieved it's over.
It wasn't so bad,
I can't wait to see everyone
Tomorrow.

Felicity Dodsley (12)
St Gabriel's School, Newbury

The First Day Of School

I felt . . .
Scared, but happy,
Nervous and excited.
What will happen?
Where will I go?
Oh no!

First lesson . . .
Maths.
I'm not very good!
What will I do?
Where will I go?

The middle of the day
Approaches fast.
Why was I worrying?
This is OK,
It isn't such a bad day.

Home at last!
What a day!
Oh great! Homework!
Lots of it!
Whoopee!
Why me?

Joanne Atkins (11)
St Gabriel's School, Newbury

The Graveyard

A broken, creaking, wooden gate
Bleak stone, grey sky
Ridged, rough ground
Ivy-covered gravestones
Ancient statues from long ago
Dismal dried flowers that weep in their sorrow
A damp, bitter breeze that sends shivers.

Grace Lake (12)
St Gabriel's School, Newbury

My First Day

Today is my first day,
How nervous and lost I feel in such a big school.
Where do I go?
Which turn do I take?
How long will I be wondering?

At last, I have found my form room,
But then,
The bell goes.
The bell is like the ring on an old milk cart.

Lessons pass;
Lunch comes.
I sit alone.
Then,
A bright face appears.
We make friends
And
Stick together the rest of the day.

Emily Cammish (11)
St Gabriel's School, Newbury

What Happens?

What happens when you leave home?
What happens when you don't hand in your homework?
What happens when you get a job?
What happens when you get your ears pierced?
What happens when you have a baby?
What happens if you have no pets?
What happens when you get braces?
What happens when you get married?
And most importantly
What happens when you don't know the answers
To these questions?

Evie Harbury (12)
St Gabriel's School, Newbury

My Boots

These are the boots,
I first waddled about in,
Finding my feet,
That rubbed my heels,
Scuffing them up,
Dusting them off.

These are the boots,
I first fell off in,
When I chose my horse
And groomed it every day,
That I polished for hours
And wouldn't let them be taken away.

These are the boots,
That keep the smile on my face,
That are my lucky charm,
The ones that scared away the monsters
And I was thankful they didn't have laces,
That I kept asking, 'Are we there yet?' in.

These are the boots,
I love and cherish,
The boots that taught me to ride,
The black, shiny boots,
I thought the world of,
The boots that put muddy footprints all over the floor.

These are the boots,
I first fell off in,
Where I caught my pony
And scraped my knee in,
These are the boots I will always remember
As my favourite boots ever.

Rhia Honey (11)
St Gabriel's School, Newbury

The Wolf

The white forests of Alaska,
Fir trees laden with snow,
What a place for creatures to live,
To eat and breed and grow.

I saw a wolf one chilling night,
While hunting rabbits and deer,
Trotting past, its ears upright,
Sensing I was near.

Abruptly stopped,
Its teeth were bared,
My heart it skipped a beat,
It gracefully turned away and snarled,
For I was not a threat.

Its emerald eyes fixated,
On a blank and snow covered space,
When another wolf pounced out of the woods,
With hatred on its face.

The wolves engaged in battle,
A territorial fight,
Scratching, snarling, biting, growling,
Each move with tremendous might.

My wolf snapped at the enemy's head,
A pitiful whine was heard,
A body fell on the bloodstained snow,
The enemy was dead!

The survivor sniffed the body,
A wretched corpse from the fray,
The wolf gave out a mighty howl
And continued on his way.

Imogen Rolfe (12)
St Gabriel's School, Newbury

The Shoes

These are the shoes,
That my dad tied up
On that very first day.
That helped me run,
Walk and play,
That I continuously
Scuffed as I fell.
That I took off
When my feet were aching.
That at the end of the day
Got chucked somewhere
But I did love those shoes!

These are the shoes,
That I strutted around in
Broadly smiling.
That took me through
Those enormous doors,
That helped me walk
Into that first lesson.
That forced me to
Go again,
But I did love those shoes!

These are the shoes,
That I came home in
Relieved it was the end of term,
That quivered almost as much
As I did, stepping through
That door,
But I did love those shoes!

Claire Wood (11)
St Gabriel's School, Newbury

Snow Tiger

Standing, a white silhouette,
Against the dark forbidding forest,
The night brings a deadly silence,
Seemingly freezing the world.

Deep black pools for eyes,
Moonlight sparkling upon them,
Like spilt gold glitter,
Falling from the moon.

Huge paws padding at the ground,
Silver fur rippling along its sides,
Movements as fluid as a trickling stream,
A shining phantom.

It has ivory white fangs,
Hidden in between its gaping jaws
And claws long and pointed,
Like sharp, unnoticeable needles.

Its eyes, discs of yellow,
Scan the hills buried deep in snow,
Looking for wandering prey,
So carelessly falling upon its path.

The shadows of prey,
Leap across the snow-laden ground,
Flitting through the twisted trees,
But not a movement from the snow tiger,
The alert, killing machine.

Alina Whitford (12)
St Gabriel's School, Newbury

My Frog Wellies

When Mum presented them to me for the first time,
I put them on and felt like a great explorer
Off I toddled into the garden
To splash in cold, frosty puddles
My idea of fun!
Falling
Crawling
Splashing
Sploshing
All of these I did in my frog wellies
Trips to farms, parks and zoos if raining
You'd find me wearing
My special frog wellies
A day of sadness came
When my feet grew
When Mum presented me
With new wellies
Plain
Green
But with *no* frog face!
I couldn't wait for summer to come
So I wouldn't have to wear my new wellies!

Isabel Rudgley (11)
St Gabriel's School, Newbury

My Feathered Friend

M ischievous
Y outhful

P ecking
A rrogant
R aucous
R owdy
O utrageous
T alkative.

Georgetta Evans (12)
St Gabriel's School, Newbury

Home Alone

Echoing
Humming
Howling
Screeching
I freeze in terror
Someone screaming
I'm rooted to the spot
I see things, I swear
Windows banging
Trees swaying
No one's there
Eyes piercing in the distance
Smells arising right up close
Running faster and faster
My feet are too tired
I dive through the air
What a thrilling scare
I've made it
I'm safe again
All tucked up in bed, right here.

Georgia Hatton-Brown (13)
St Gabriel's School, Newbury

Sheep

Sheep
On a hill
Always grazing
White woolly coat
Feeding happily
A car!
Panic struck
It runs away
Sadness at the disturbed tranquillity.

Charlotte Osborne (12)
St Gabriel's School, Newbury

Midnight Dancers

Running, frolicking
Two of them dancing
White socks flashing
In the moon's beam
Eyes full of fun
Eyes full of play
A rabbit runs
Across the field
The dancing stops
Ears pricked
Eyes searching
The coast is clear
And on with the dancing
Cantering, bucking
In perfect synchrony
So elegant
So graceful
How I love my midnight dancers.

Becky Weeks (12)
St Gabriel's School, Newbury

The Key To My Heart

The key to my heart is:

The sound of a bouncing baby boy laughing
Snow crunching underneath my boots
The sound of waves crashing on the rocks

The taste of treacle sponge drenched in golden syrup
The oozing taste of chocolate melting in my mouth
Ice cream on a hot summer's day melting down my hand

The key to my heart is:

The touch of squidgy sand between my toes
The cosy duvet on my bed
My dog's wet nose against my hand
And of course, my cuddly toy, Lenny the lion!

Danielle Johnson (12)
St Gabriel's School, Newbury

Tiger

Tiger sitting in the wet grass
Looks asleep
His eyes flicker

He stalks
The zebra looks
Watching
He licks his lips

His eyes are green
And staring
His tail flicks
Coat glistening

Lonely . . .
Hungry . . .
Waiting . . .
Watching . . .

Sophie Fowler (12)
St Gabriel's School, Newbury

Cat

By my bed,
A shadow lurks,
A creeping noise,
A flicker of light.
Lime-green eyes,
Shine so bright.
Its silky coat,
Black as night,
Black as ninja.
Agile ninja.
Fighting the darkness . . .
Creeping . . .
Watching . . .
Lingering and knowing.
It's taunting me until dawn!

Bianca Rodriguez (12)
St Gabriel's School, Newbury

Cynophobia

Cynophobia
My fear of dogs
It's really very strange
Any dogs,
Big or small,
I'm scared of every one,
I think they're cute,
When they are still,
But when they run,
I freak,
Cynophobia,
My fear of dogs,
It's been there since I was three.

Charlotte Phelps (12)
St Gabriel's School, Newbury

Hallowe'en

Walking
In the dark
Trees swaying
Owls hooting
The smell of burning all around us
Walking along the road
Hallowe'en costumes dragging behind

My friend and I anxiously look around
Nothing!
We carry on walking
'There's something there, I swear!'
Turning round very, very slowly
Argh!
There, standing in front of us
Underneath a long, black, hooded cloak
Stands . . .

My brother!

Jessica Townend (12)
St Gabriel's School, Newbury

The Secrets Inside

The secrets inside . . .
    Hiccupping horses feeling happy,
    A smooth sunset shimmering at night
    A pink stiletto shining in the sky.

The secrets inside . . .
    Licking my lips from salty crackling,
    A toffee stuck to my teeth,
    Sour taste of lemon sizzling in my mouth.

The secrets inside . . .
    Galloping horses along the beach,
    The sight of melting chocolate,
    A bee buzzing around.

The secrets inside . . .
    The warming touch of a horse's nose,
    A silk Chinese dress in my hands,
    The wind blowing through my hair.

The secrets inside . . .

Georgia Robertson (12)
St Gabriel's School, Newbury

The Gymnast

There she is, flipping so much, you lose count,
Then, leaping into the sky, gracefully,
Spinning like a ballerina,
Running quicker than lightning,
Tossing and turning,
Springing up and down,
Somersaulting in the air, elegantly,
Stretching to the limit,
Tumbling with joy,
Walking back home,
All of this, just to get to the top.

Melanie Davies (12)
St Gabriel's School, Newbury

Diamonds And Rubies

What diamonds are made of

The swishing sea of the Equator
The hiccupping heat of Dubai
The wicked wind of the west

In my box I have

The sweet taste of pancakes with sugar and lemon
The crunchy taste of doughnuts hitting my mouth
The thought of Easter eggs melting in my mouth

In my special box I have
The smell of Coco Chanel touching my wrist
The crisp smell of a winter day
The smell of sea shells on the seashore.

Hannah Sutton (13)
St Gabriel's School, Newbury

My First Shoes

My first shoes are the ones
I fell over in, the ones I learnt
To walk and run in.

My first shoes turned from
Blue to brown
As I fell and tripped and ran.

My first shoes let me climb
And play in the sun all day long
I had no time to rest
But by the end of the day, I was a cheeky mess.

My first shoes at the end of the day
Would fall asleep in my wardrobe
Looking forward to the next exciting day.

Sarah Warwick (11)
St Gabriel's School, Newbury

Special Little Wonders

My special wonders are:

The tangy taste of toffee
Crumbling caramel biscuits crunching in my mouth
Sand seeping through my toes on a beach

My special wonders are:

The taste of gooey caramel that sticks to my mouth
Thick, runny tomato soup slithering warmly down my throat
Creamy chocolate melting on my tongue

My special wonders are:

The rain in the winter
The shine in the summer
Gold that glitters on your heart

My special wonders are:

The soft touch of new clothes
Pearls that shine in the moonlight
Ice frozen in a white masterpiece
And all the charms of the world!

Eleanor Baxter (12)
St Gabriel's School, Newbury

Autumn Days

Autumn leaves cover the garden,
Wonderful, beautiful colours,
Warm and cosy, happy faces,
Snuggled in scarf and hat,
Chasing games, building dens,
Stamping feet, crunching sounds,
Home at last, lovely family,
Curled by the hot fireplace,
End of an amazing day!

Emily Westcar (11)
St Gabriel's School, Newbury

My Shoes

These are the shoes,
I got when I was five,
That I ran around the house in,
I wore to school every day.

These are the shoes,
That I went to town in,
I wore to parties,
That I adored so much.

These were my favourite shoes;
They sit there still,
In their box,
In the cupboard.

I look at them often,
Not daring to lift the lid more than an inch,
They're still undamaged and perfect,
Their glitter still sparkles bright.

Katherine Emo (12)
St Gabriel's School, Newbury

Hippo

His name is Hippo
My maid in Dubai
Gave him to me in difficult times.
Each day I would go into her room
To ask to play with him.
I spent hours in my room talking to him,
About friends,
About questions,
About worries.
Hippo is my best friend.
He still sits on my desk
Patiently waiting, for the next question.

Holly Hall (11)
St Gabriel's School, Newbury

Teddy

This is the teddy
That lived in my bed,
That lost an eye long ago.
His brown woolly fur
And little leather paws
Have fallen apart
Through love.
This was the teddy
That was mended
By Grandma
And made
A snug purple suit.
This is the teddy
Who travels the world,
Who wears boxer shorts
But still loves me best.
This is the teddy that nearly
Lived in a box
But decided against it
So he'll always live in my bed.
This is the teddy
Who was bullied by friends
And told his head was too big
But at night
I told him, 'No worries.'
This is the teddy
Who is the best
That can't be beaten
Who will always
Love me.

Lucy Wildsmith (11)
St Gabriel's School, Newbury

Teddy

This is the teddy that I love the most
He used to be white
But now he's gone cream
He has big green eyes
That are covered in fur
I've cried my eyes out
Cuddled close to him
I've told him
All my deepest, darkest secrets
Because I know he won't tell
He's gone everywhere with me
Down to Cornwall
And across the sea
I love him so much
I can't imagine life without him
He used to come with me
On every outing
When I grow old
I'll keep him with me
Forever and ever
Just him and me.

Beth Nichol (11)
St Gabriel's School, Newbury

The Golden Sunflower

Sunflowers climb up the bare wall
Their smooth stalks make pathways to Heaven
As they stretch up even further.

Suddenly, golden light floods
The creation gently opens up
Soft, yellow petals warm up hearts and souls.

But these delicate plants' journey is almost over
Carefully, they twist back down to Earth.

Fiona Muir (12)
St Gabriel's School, Newbury

My Cat

This is the cat
I've always had
Her name is Jess
The black and white puss
She's the cat from Postman Pat
But she's not Pat's
She's mine, all mine.

Her whispery fur
Is as black as night
And the white
As blank as a page
Her eyes are as green
As emeralds and grass
Yes, she's mine, all mine.

I took her everywhere I went
She flew down the slides
Gliding happily and free
She snuggles in with me at night in bed
I'm happy to know
She's mine, all mine.

Once, I left her at a hotel
I cried and cried and cried
But when she bounced back
Into my reaching arms
She was mine, all mine.

I still have Jess at home with me
She's not been on many adventures lately
But I know in my heart
(And Jess knows it too!)
That she's mine, just mine.

Miranda Porter (12)
St Gabriel's School, Newbury

My Teddy

This is the teddy I've had since I was born
He's been stroked and cuddled
And hugged all my life
He's touched my face
He's touched my hand
I hug him and he hugs me.
Once he'd been loved a couple of years
He began to get holes all over his body
His stuffing came out
So I made him a suit.
When I have my teddy
I suck my thumb
When I sleep in bed
He's nice and warm
And makes me feel safe.
Once I left him at nursery
In a toolbox upstairs
I cried and cried all night long.
My teddy is 11, quite old now!
But all those years
He's smiled and smiled
And I know he is meant for me.

Chloe Veal (11)
St Gabriel's School, Newbury

My Dress

This is the dress I wore
When I had my first Holy Communion.
When my mum smiled at me
When my gran said she was proud of me
When I held a lit candle
When I felt like an angel
When I took the bread and wine
And afterwards said my prayers.
When I was nervous that I would forget my lines
Because they were in Ukrainian.
When I felt special
When I smiled all day
When I had a huge party afterwards.

This is the dress I wore
That is still hanging in my cupboard
That I will never wear again
That still looks beautiful
That is still pure white with delicate pearls
That I am now only ever going to wear in the photos
That will not fit me anymore.

This is the dress I will never forget.

Larissa Hawkins (11)
St Gabriel's School, Newbury

Harold

This is the teddy
I love and cherish,
That is old and bald
And very fragile,
This is the teddy
That sleeps with me at night.

This is the teddy
That is 11 years old,
Arms are floppy
Head is wonky,
This is the teddy
That has his own chair.

This is the teddy
That has little clothes,
Knitted by Grandma
With love and with care,
The teddy that has been everywhere
And his name is Harold.

Alice Martin (11)
St Gabriel's School, Newbury

Ocean

Golden sand upon beach
Fish dart and play through coral,
Predators, prey, sharks and jellyfish
The waves roll like a puppy with a toy,
Fishermen with nets full of fish
Life, colour and creation all in the ocean.

Monsters dwell twenty thousand leagues
Whilst submarines head to war,
Near the surface, mer-people play
Undiscovered caves lay forgotten,
All this in the seven seas.

Antonia Wong (11)
St Gabriel's School, Newbury

These Are The Jodhpurs

These are the jodhpurs
I rode around in.
Had my first canter
Jumped my first jump in
And smiled
My biggest smile in.
These are the jodhpurs
I trotted, jumped and cantered in,
That I wore when
I won my first show,
Had my first fall.
These are the jodhpurs
All tattered and faded
I wore so much
And are so lucky.
These they are
Safely in the cupboard.

Chloe Watson-Smith (11)
St Gabriel's School, Newbury

The South Tower Library!

We sat in the library
In front of the happy tree,
Smiling down at us,
Mummy, Helena and me!
Reading books together on Barbie!
We had a feeling of safety
Not wanting to go home,
Not wanting to leave.
Just wanting to stay and read!
Now years later, I remember the moment
I was told of the tragedy.
Remembering how I'd enjoyed that place
Never again would I sit under that tree!

Maddy Rowley (11)
St Gabriel's School, Newbury

My Swimming Costume

This is the swimming costume I wore when I . . .
Learned to swim
I splashed my mum
I paddled in rock pools
Got bitten by crabs.

This is the swimming costume I wore when I . . .
Buried my sleeping dad
I built my first sandcastle
I jumped in the pool.

This is the swimming costume I wore when I . . .
Got some goggles and went under water
I wailed for *another* ice cream.

Now it is in the cupboard
It looks dejected and alone
Now it is left to rest
Not moving until . . .

Amy Hopes (11)
St Gabriel's School, Newbury

These Are The Shoes

These are the shoes
I thumped around in
Whirled and twirled
And flew up high in
The princess pink satin
With long string laces
My fairy wings matched
With glitter and sequins
The gentle *tink-tink*
Of the piano shadowing
Our footsteps.
Until my chubby feet refused to fit!
A dancing legend lost forever!

Georgie Byfield (11)
St Gabriel's School, Newbury

My Ballet Shoes

These are the shoes,
I first ever danced in,
Bought for my second birthday
Clean, white and silky,
With one elastic strap,
Uncomfy at first,
Then worn proudly by me!
One ribbon at the front
I could never tie
They went through my first exam,
When I grew out of them
Loudly did I cry,
But the cupboard has them now
With dust on the strap,
I will cherish them forever.

Rebecca Whittaker (11)
St Gabriel's School, Newbury

Fire

Creeping quietly through the sleeping house,
The deadly beast with smoky breath,
A flickering tongue,
Teeth that bite all in its path.

Stealthily it moves,
Flames licking the walls,
Foul breath poisoning the house.

Growing in confidence,
Chomping up the furniture,
Proudly gnawing at the stairs.

Finally, tired
The beast begins to die,
Nothing is left . . .

Daisy Morley (11)
St Gabriel's School, Newbury

Winter

Snowflakes falling, dancing round and round
Touching my eyes and nose as I frown.
The carol singers gather round the door,
Their lovely voices rise and fall, I long for more.

Hurrah! Santa's coming, my stocking's ready,
It's Christmas Eve and I must keep myself steady.
Will there be a big bulge on top of my sheet,
If I stay fast asleep and don't wiggle my feet.

Goodness, am I lucky enough to find some gifts?
My heart is leaping and I feel such a lift.
There are the presents, ranged under the tree,
Could they really all be waiting for me?

But, this is Christmas Day, time for church,
However, some do not worship, they search and search.
What can baby Jesus have brought to this land?
Could peace and goodwill really live hand in hand?

Let us remember those who have no meals,
As we eat and drink and our laughter peals.
When we feel gloomy and dismal under winter's gloom,
We know the spring light will come again into our room.

Lily Rolfe (11)
St Gabriel's School, Newbury

My First Coat

This was my first coat that kept me warm in the cold winter
And autumn breeze, which kept me from freezing
This could fill me with a warm glow
That would flow from top to toe

Where I could be warm
And away from the cold
It was pink and fluffy
And when I put it on, I would not take it off
So my dad used to gently prise it off me

Soft and cosy
And it was my own
It was a perfect fit
The others were dull and boring black, white and grey
But this was pink and white
My favourite colours at the time

Everyone used to stare at me as I slowly disappeared
Into the comfort of my coat
It was like no other
You could say it was one of a kind
That's because it's mine.

Olivia Shotliff (11)
St Gabriel's School, Newbury

My Poem

The cold, rough sea
Swept in the stone,
Smooth
Not jagged
All left alone

It was beautiful
Dazzling
Magnificent

It took my breath away

I picked it up
Slid it on some string
And kept it forever
In my dreams.

Joanna Ash (13)
St Gabriel's School, Newbury

Worms

Soft, cushiony, yielding to a prod,
Pink, like newborn creatures,
Just alive,
But also like wrinkly old grannies and grandads,
Puckered, pleated and crumpled,
Slender, lean, with ends identical,
Soiled, particles attached to damp flesh,
Ridges, evenly spread, like ruler lines, regular,
Lengthy, as unending as streamers curling round.

Twisting, zigzagging through moist soil,
Like mobile caravans, always on the move,
Proceeding, not knowing what lies ahead,
Pausing, sensing trouble, withering,
Enemy approaches, writhe, withdraw,
Curl up, still, stationary.

Charity Rankin (12)
St Gabriel's School, Newbury

Fire

The demon rushes, torching everything in sight
It spits
It roars
As it brushes past
Shrieks at the ashes left behind
Scalds you inside out
Yells as it burns
Doesn't care about anything else
Everything seems inconvenient
Compared to the mass of heat itself
Grows on youth, learns from age
And becomes uncontrollable
Loves to hate, hates to love
And so it destroys everything.

Leila Zarazel (12)
St Gabriel's School, Newbury

The Desert

Here he is so far from people,
Trapped here and unable to walk,
Too vast to fit in,
He is Hell for everyone.

Murders people who approach nearby,
You'll turn crazy if you come near,
Thirst, then death, will overcome you,
His uncontrolled power will haunt you forever.

His heart wounded . . . so unloved,
His golden body creeps up on you,
Friendless . . . he is,
Hurt . . . he is,
Ocean of fire . . . he is!

Kimberly Ann Corrios Maravillas (13)
St Gabriel's School, Newbury

Lost In The Ocean

I entered the arch-shape door,
I trembled nervously,
Thinking I was going to do something wrong.
I felt like water,
Streaming down as if I were leaving this world,
Flowing to the ocean,
Lost in the ocean.
The wind blew into my face,
Making me cold,
Making me fear more.
Then, my head went up,
I heard this voice,
The voice I've known for a long time!
She turned and looked at me,
Smiled,
It was her!
I knew I was alone no more,
No longer lost in the ocean.

Harriet Carver (11)
St Gabriel's School, Newbury

Conkers

Conkers, giant conkers,
Conkers are such fun,
In the autumn afternoon,
They glisten in the sun.

Conker wars in the morning,
Conker wars at night,
I must find the perfect one,
My conker must be right.

Conkers, I love conkers,
I've found the perfect one,
But now conkers are all over,
Winter's just begun.

Stephanie Snelling (11)
St Gabriel's School, Newbury

The Countryside

The swerving country lanes
Winding in and out the dusty hills.

Rivers running through the valleys
In the remote countryside.

Wild deer roaming through
The old swaying trees.

Sheep grazing in a nearby field
Munching away all day long.

Fields and fields of long grass
Swishing in the wind.

This is what the countryside is like
And no one can ever change that.

Ella Nicklin (11)
St Gabriel's School, Newbury

Dandelion Clock

Tiny little dandelion clock,
Blowing in the breeze,
Like a fairy prancing and dancing
In the summer sun.

Unexpectedly, the wind picks up speed,
Poor little dandelion,
Pushed higher and higher,
Soaring through the tree tops
Like a shimmer of light illuminating the air.

Suddenly, the dandelion clock's head goes bare,
Like a fairy sprinkling fairy dust from her magic pouch
Across the sky,
Poor little dandelion quivering in the chill
Of the midsummer sun.

Emma James-Crook (13)
St Gabriel's School, Newbury

Forgotten Hamster

Stuffed on a bookshelf
In an old, tatty cage
Alone
Scared
Waiting
Watching
Hoping
Eyes filled with tears
A creak at the door
A movement within
Tapping at the cage
Hoping they'll hear
Remember
Care
Begging . . .
For warmth
Food
Help.

Hannah Miles (12)
St Gabriel's School, Newbury

The Night Sky

He comes slowly, creeping over the sky,
Until he is there, in his full, black glory.
But the children are sleeping, not to see him,
The rest of the world can see nothing.

All of a sudden, he twinkles with stardust,
Finally, the moon wanders into sight.
So the world can see again,
They bathe in his beauty.

Once people have had a long look at him,
He puts them all to sleep
And waits for the last person to snore,
Finally, enjoying the view himself.

Lucy Blanchard (13)
St Gabriel's School, Newbury

The Storm

Lightning lit the black sky
For a split second,
Thunder pounded
High in the sky,
Rain bounced off the rooftops
And into the overflowing gutters

The sea crashed on the shore,
Waves broken by sharp rocks,
Ships battered and sails torn
As the ocean was out of control

Howling, gale force winds
Like a hurricane,
Trees falling all around,
Plants crushed by the force,
Power lost
In the darkness of the night

Sudden stillness,
The wind stopped howling
Rain stopped flooding,
A ray of light coming from the east
Sun began to emerge,
Erasing memory of previous night,
Wildlife out from hiding,
Birds sand,
Everyone was happy,
The new day had come.

Annabel Hawkesworth (13)
St Gabriel's School, Newbury

Sunset

The sky turns into a fiery blaze,
As if it had been set alight.
Shadows stretch like elastic,
As far as they can go.
The sun slowly sinks,
Singeing the tops of trees,
Transforming the grass,
Into beautiful blades of glistening gold.
Birds sing softly and sweetly,
Their lullaby to the animal kingdom.
Sending the world into a silent slumber.
Small children's curtains close,
As their parents tuck them into bed,
Whilst the moon wakes up,
Taking the many stars with him, into the sky.
Suddenly, the sun slips
And falls down from the horizon
And we are plunged once more,
Into a pool of icy darkness.

Emily Anderson (12)
St Gabriel's School, Newbury

Wouldn't It Be Nice To Be A Cat?

Wouldn't it be nice to be a cat?

You can lounge all day on a comfy sofa,
Pounce around the house like it's all yours.
You can show off by climbing a great big tree
And hope that cats really do land on their four paws.

You might want to try and catch the fluttering butterflies,
Stalk around in the long, wet grass.
You could jump up onto the fence to see the view
And watch the beautiful singing birds fly pass.

You can sneak next door into their garden,
Go and act smooth in front of the other local cats.
You might want to clamber into the mysterious farm barn
And chase around the squeaking bats.

And after a long, tiring day,
You can go back to your home and family.
Snuggle up in your owner's welcoming bed
And purr there very quietly.

So, don't you think it would be nice to be a cat?

Luisa Boheimer (13)
St Gabriel's School, Newbury

Sunnie

My comfort in summer,
My friend in winter,
My blossom in spring,
My star in autumn.
As bright as the sun,
As sweet as daisies,
As white as snow,
As pure as ice.
As pretty as petals,
As precious as pearls,
As fresh as dew,
As fast as the river.

She pushingly purrs at me for food,
Like a bossy herring gull!
She follows me around,
Like ducklings following their mother.
She enthusiastically eats my dinner behind my back,
Like a cheeky chimp stealing bananas.

She struts around my bedroom as if it was hers,
She foolishly frightens herself, by watching the claws of shadows.
Until I instantly appear looking for her,
She suddenly jumps into my arms.
In the evening, she comfortably curls up, asleep on my bed,
Awaiting the forgiving footsteps of night, ringing in her ears.

Natasha Hookings (12)
St Gabriel's School, Newbury

Four Seasons

Pink buds, green leaves,
Rabbits ears'
Like jumping jacks, hop through the long, green grass.

Sweltering sun, swaying breeze,
Deckchairs lined on the beach,
Like a stripy suit convention.

Rainbow leaves, harvest time,
The nights draw in,
Like curtains closing in on the day.

Soft snow, Christmas presents,
The homely fire blazes through the house,
Like the twinkle of the fairy lights.

Elizabeth Hughes (12)
St Gabriel's School, Newbury

The Gibbon

Graham the gibbon
Wears a pale brown ribbon.
He is furry and soft
And lives in a loft.

Katie Thorne (13)
The Castle School

Pansy The Monkey

I am black and teeny.
I am happy and weeny.
My name is Pansy
And I love eating candy.

Scott Yeates (11)
The Castle School

Polo

He lives in the North Pole.
He went for a walk.
It was cold and snowy, the wind all blowy.
He is black and white with a red bow.
He wore it round his neck so that he was seen in the snow.

Faye Douglas (12)
The Castle School

Snaky

He has got a long tongue and a slippery, stretchy body.
A very loud hiss and can knock you down.
He is green, yellow and black.

He is cheesy and smelly and will bite you if you touch him.
He is very fast and can wiggle quickly.
He likes to eat bears and worms.

Haddon Macdonald (12)
The Castle School

George

He plays with his brothers until dusk.
Mum says, 'Bath time George.'
Then he goes to brush his teeth.
His mum says, 'You have been good so,
I'll let you go to the park tomorrow.'

Simon Ball (11)
The Castle School

What Am I?

I come in different breeds.
I can be different sizes.
I have a wagging tail.
I have fur.
I live in some people's houses.
I have a bed of my own.
I usually have sharp teeth
And claws.
I can be lots of colours.
I am quite loud.
I have four legs.
What am I?

Monty Morgan (12)
The Clere School

What Am I?

I like the dark.
I love eating rodents.
I don't like light.
I can't see.
I have fur like bears' fur.
I have a high-pitched squeak,
like the chalk on a blackboard.
I have claws like a pin.
I move upside down.

Alex Brown (12)
The Clere School

School

School is cool,
or so I thought
until one day,
in a test I got nought.
Since that day,
I've gone down and down,
so now when I see it
I always wear a frown.

Hannah Best (11)
The Clere School

Watership Down

As you look at Watership Down the sheep just look like balls of wool,
you just wish you could reach out and touch them, grab them with
your silky hands, coil your fingers round the newborn lambs.

As you look at Watership Down, the trees are as green as green,
The leaves are scattered everywhere by people on a country walk;
By the farmer and his little black collie, scouring the hills for the sight
of a fox.

Sophie Elgar (11)
The Clere School

What Am I?

I'm like the snowy plains of Russia.
I am a predator.
I wait for the lonely deer.
I'll pull your sleigh if you tame me;
But, I'm wild, I'm fluffy but evil,
I call out on the cliff tops.

Jamie Miles (12)
The Clere School

What Am I?

I'll give you a clue of what I am.
I'm a rodent.
I come in many different colours,
Like brown, white and even ginger.
My teeth are sharp like blades.
My eyes are marbles.
I squeak like a mouse
But I can assure you I'm not a mouse.
My claws are sharp like needles.
I have soft silky fur.
I eat fruit and vegetables.
I can live indoors or out.

What am I?

Fern Dabill (12)
The Clere School

What Am I?

I am smaller than a thumb nail.
I build my own home.
I move not too slowly and not too fast.
I eat flower petals and eat leaves.
I eat as I travel or I eat in my home.
As I cry, I make no sound.
I move faster than a snail
But slower than a human walking.
I can go into tub containers.
My eyes are smaller than the tip of a needle.

What am I?

Alexandra McGlone (12)
The Clere School

The Goal

The crowd was going wild,
It was like a lion's roar.
Steven Gerrard stepped up
And he wanted to score.

The wind was blowing violently,
The stars were shining bright
But Liverpool FC
Were still winning on the night.

As Stevie G ran up step by step,
The Red's fans quietened down,
And as Gerrard made contact
A hush ran through the ground.

Travelling like a rocket
The ball was firmly met,
The keeper couldn't save it
And it hit the back of the net.

It was now three-one to the Reds
With ninety minutes gone,
Now the Liverpool fans
Started singing a song.

James Bowman (11)
The Clere School

What Am I?

My body is slimy and streamlined.
I come in lots of different species.
Some people fear me because I kill in such a surprising way.
I have rows of teeth like shattered glass.
I am one of the most feared predators in the world.
I have a scarred face from when I've been in close encounters
with my other species.

What am I?

Jack Andrews (12)
The Clere School

Autumn In England And Pakistan

The light
The shining sun
Slowly shivers a spark down my spine.
My friends have arrived in their car now.
I wave to them, rushing my warm buttered toast.
They shout, 'Hurry or we'll miss school!'
As I rush to get dressed and grab my bag!

The darkness
The thumping thunder
Rips a shiver down my aching spine.
The food truck's arrived,
We stumble over to it with hearts filled with hope!
The smell if rice makes our eyes water.
We huddle shouting furiously for a bag of rice
And a bottle of water to keep us going!

Meghan Capewell (11)
The Clere School

What Am I?

My skin is rough as rock.
I can run up to forty miles per hour.
I am strong, like a tree.
My home is rough, dusty and hot.
I am quite plump like a whale.
I can get very mad like a wasp.
There is not very much of me.
I can live in a zoo.
I look old but I am not.
I get in loads of fights like a lion.

What am I?

Samantha North (12)
The Clere School

Year Seasons

Frosty grass
Steamed up glass
Autumn time is
Coming in.

Rain, hail,
Snow and wind
Wintertime is
Coming in.

Green, green grass
Is coming then
Springtime is
Coming in.

Sunny days
Hot and long
Summertime is
Coming in.

Frosty grass
Steamed up glass
Autumn time is
Coming in.

George Dyer (11)
The Clere School

What Am I?

My eyes are buttonholes.
My skin, sleek and smooth like a snake.
My tongue, slimy like a snake and long like a snake;
But I am not a snake.
I have no cry, I am silent like a rabbit.
I scuttle up trees, fast as a hare
Darting from branch to branch, searching for food.
You may not see me, as I am small and can hide myself.

Corinne Taylor (12)
The Clere School

Rules, Rules, Rules

There are rules about everything I suppose,
Rules even for picking your nose.
Rules for games and rules for sports
Even for buttoning tops and shorts!

*Rules, rules - they make you sad,
And don't they completely drive you mad?*

Rules at home, at work at play,
Rules during the night and day.
Don't do this! But please do that!
Stroke your dog and feed the cat.

*Rules, rules - they make you sad,
And don't they completely drive you mad?*

Wash your hands and comb your hair,
You can look at her but do not stare.
This homework must be in on time -
And don't forget to make it rhyme!

*Rules, rules - they make you sad,
And don't they completely drive you mad?*

Sam Price (11)
The Clere School

What Am I?

My coat is as soft as a bear.
I wake up at night and drive people crazy
          running around in my wheel.
I eat veg and dry food.
I'm scared of my enemies - *miaow;*
But I'm safe behind bars.

What am I?

Tara Lewis (13)
The Clere School

Winter's Coming!

Chilly mornings, mist lingers,
I can hardly feel my fingers.

Glistening cobwebs, apples drop,
As I wait at the cold bus stop.

Leaves falling, wind blows,
I stamp my feet and wiggle my toes.

Giant pumpkins, trick or treat,
Something warm at home to eat.

Gleaming conkers, shining bright,
It won't be long till Bonfire Night.

Hat and scarf, street lamps glowing,
There may be a chance that it starts snowing.

Frosty grass, early night,
Soon the bus will be in my sight.

Headlights blinding, bus is here,
I know that winter is very near.

Matthew Lawrence (11)
The Clere School

Cheese

Cheese, cheese the wonderful stuff,
Some people just can't get enough.
It can come with holes or maybe mould,
And normal people just eat it cold.
When it's old it goes horribly smelly,
Just like a sweaty old dirty wellie.
Kids should eat it, it will make them grow strong.
It's so great, it makes me break into song.

Ben Rampton (12)
The Clere School

People All Around The World

So many people all around the world,
Some with straight hair, some with curls,
Some with black hair, some with blonde,
All around the world singing songs.

Dancing people all around the world,
Dancing, dancing, come on girls,
Swirling, swirling round and round,
Come on boys, come dance around.

Singing people all around the world,
Singing and waving flags unfurled,
Ducking and diving round about,
Come on people, give us a *shout!*

Katie Scott (11)
The Clere School

Friendship

Friendship is all I need
To get me through the day.
I laugh, I talk, I play.

Friendship is all about sharing
Your hopes and dreams.
Helping each other through
All life's twists and turns.

Friendship isn't always easy,
Friends can let you down,
But good friends last forever
And try to stick around.

Susan Connor (11)
The Clere School

The Hunted

Eyes of fury,
Talons of destruction,
Confidence of a thundering knight.
Misery awaits.

Death covers talons,
Sorrowful winds of sadness,
Clouds of help surround.

Ready to shoot,
Speeding bullets of fury,
Destruction attacks.

Furious talons,
Predators wait to attack,
Death awaits for all.

Joshua Adamson (11)
The Clere School

Pets Aren't Worth It!

In the night, in a dark wood,
There was a woman crying like anyone would.
She was crying because her dog had died,
He tripped over a wire and got fried.
So on the floor the poor dog lay,
Oh why oh why did that dog get fried.
On the pavement the dog lay roasted,
Although I'm sure she didn't want him toasted.

In the morning on a sunny day,
Cat insurance she forgot to pay.
Oh, when that cat was sniffing up a tree,
He fell and squashed all his fleas.
So my advice to you is don't get pets,
Or you will always be at the vet's!

Luke Otton (12)
The Clere School

Prehistoric World Dining Room

The light is the soft glow of the early evening sun.
The table is a giant mammoth grazing on the grass with its long,
hairy trunk.
The brown carpet is the soft, moist earth beneath the mammoth's
massive feet.
The chairs are a pack of vicious sabre-tooth cats preparing to pounce
on the unwary mammoth.
The bookcase is a gigantic indricothere browsing on the top of a lush,
green tree.
The TV is a doedicurus male, which has been battered into
submission during the mating season.
I am tucking in the chairs now; the cats pounce on the mammoth with
lightning speed.
I am going out and turning off the light; the sun goes down and
darkness falls.
The animals lie down and go to sleep.

Jaimie Schenkelaars (11)
The Clere School

Ice Skating

It's cold in the rink,
The music blasts loud,
There's a thrill in the skater,
Doing her elegant spin.

There's a triumph in the air
As she does a big jump
And lands in a beautiful pose.

The music comes to an end,
The crowd starts to cheer,
There's that thrill in the skater
As she smiles and bows.

Laura Skinner (11)
The Clere School

Books

Books make you get hooked,
Hooked on reading,
Reading being tempting,
Tempting to read all day.
Day passes by too quickly,
Quickly you need to read,
Read good books and bad books.
Books make me go quiet,
Quiet lets you read,
Read big books and small books.
Books make me feel light,
Light that floats away,
Away I fly to a different land,
Land of faraway.
Away I go into my book,
Book that makes me dream,
Dreams of peace,
Peace that is not broken.
Broken peace lead to war,
War that never ends.
End of books makes me sad,
Sad that always returns,
Returns when I finish my book.
Book started again,
Again I go into a different land,
Land of faraway.
Away I fly into my book,
Book of peace and freedom,
Freedom is how I feel,
I feel when reading books.

Sam Ingrorsen (11)
The Clere School

The Mouse

While I was lying in my bed,
Dreaming, fast asleep.
I felt tickly, tiny toes
On tickly, tiny feet.
When I looked up
There were teeny, tiny, muddy footprints
Across my brand-new sheet.

I scanned my bedroom floor
And then along the wall,
I wasn't completely sure
What ran across my feet
And spoiled my brand-new sheet.

Then I saw it,
A long, raw, scabby tail,
Whiskers like rusted wire;
A terrible mousy stink was filling up the room.
I had to get out quick or else I would be sick.
I ran along the carpet but got beaten by the mouse.
He must have supersonic strength to slam the door that fast.

I was trapped. Nowhere to go, nowhere to hide
The mouse's back was straight with pride.
I ran to the safety of my bed and raised my pillow above my head
With one mighty swing at the mouse - I missed.
It squealed one deafening screeching hiss.
This left me sprawled upon my bed
And wishing that blasted mouse was dead!

Emma Sygrove-Savill (12)
The Clere School

Shoes, Shoes

Shoes, shoes lovely shoes,
How can I afford them all?
Russell and Bromley, Barrett's, Clarks
They're all down in the mall.

All different colours, plain or bright,
Red, orange, pink or brown.
They're all my favourite colour shoes,
You can find them all in town!

My favourite shoes are stiletto boots,
Any colour will do.
You can show them off at any time,
Even when you're in the loo!

Now you've found out my favourite shoes,
I hope you will take my advice.
Now go out and show them off girl,
And definitely don't think twice!

Cloé Higgs (11)
The Clere School

My Pets

For my twelfth birthday I got some fish
Which will never be used as a teatime dish.

I've also got some Aylesbury ducks
That mess around in the mud and the muck.

Our two dogs like to go out for a run
Especially in the hot summer's sun.

We have several chickens that lay small eggs
Which we sometimes use to make ourselves cakes.

The cat that we have sometimes catches mice
Which he brings to the house (doesn't look very nice).

Chris Prozzo (12)
The Clere School

The Cat

I have a friend
Who's just round the corner.
As thick as a tree trunk
Her name is Laura.
She's just been to town
And look what she's found . . .
It's a great big pussycat!
She brought him home,
He looked quite alone.
So she brought him some company,
A big gruff dog.
Sweet and pathetic, his name is Mog!
We kept them a while
Till it go too vile.
So we dumped them on the street
Then they met a bird - *tweet-tweet!*

Kimberley Hutton (12)
The Clere School

The Cat-Fish

I had never seen a goldfish that size
With big yellow teeth and black beady eyes.
On the carpet yes I lie
For lunch the fish, or blueberry pie.
Slowly up to the fish I spy
A body of stripes like a tie.
I pounce before the time is nigh
Only to find myself miaowing - bye
Little did I know that I would die
The harmless goldfish took my last life.

Bethany Lawrence (12)
The Clere School

Betty The Pink-Nosed Cow

Betty was an average cow except for her pink nose,
She had a white coat with black spots, the only clothes she chose.
But one day Betty wasn't there, she's vanished in the air.
All the other cows grinded their food,
When I heard something make a thundering moo!
I stood, I stared, I was very, very scared,
A huge brown blob trenched towards me.
Its nose dripping with snot, as gooey as goo
Still standing there
I saw its eerie eyes cringe at me.
'Betty, it that you?' I stuttered.
But all it did was moo!
And its spots like bottomless pits of evil slurped me into
Splodges of green cud.
Her tail was furry and fat
Now a skeleton, none of that.
Steam came out of her nose, hot, cold and smelly.
The best of her chipped hooves, ready to move.
She backed away.
Finally I stood, I stared, I wasn't very scared.
Betty was as normal as could be
But sometimes she attempts to storm at me.
But it doesn't bother me, nor do I mind
Because I know I'm just going to see her behind.

Jess Walford (12)
The Clere School

My Parrot With An Attitude

Have you ever met a parrot with an attitude,
That doesn't give you any gratitude.
When you give him food
He is so rude.
The day he went mad
I was extremely sad.
He flapped his wings with rage,
Constantly bashing his beak on his cage.
His wings are so frightening,
When he flies like lightning.
He swooped down,
Then grabbed my toy clown.
He shredded it with his claws,
For that he needed no applause.
His squawk
Is like a bad-tempered hawk.
He bites and he fights,
And he reaches great heights,
To then swoop down upon my head,
Where he scratches and pecks.
What can I do next
With a parrot with attitude
That is so rude?

Sean Hills (12)
The Clere School

The Sheep

Every day and every night,
People will be watched in daylight
By a mysterious creature,
Which is very dangerous.
A tongue like a razor,
Wool as sharp as a knife.
The way his eyes gleam,
The way his eyes zoom in.
One quick kick will make you
Crack like a piece of glass.
Every morning when people pass,
He acts innocent and eats a piece of grass.
But actually he eats people.
Then one day a man poisoned himself
So the animal died
But something mysterious happened
And no one knows what.

Jack Hibberd (13)
The Clere School

What Am I?

I stalk you through the weeds,
Of this pain-filled world.
While searching for food and water.
I spot you through the corner of my eye.
Pouncing like a gazelle,
I take you out.
Slowly killing you with gut-wrenching jaws.
Getting away from scavengers,
I leap up a tree,
Using my dagger-like claws
To cling on.
In peace, I rip you apart.

Gareth Wardhaugh (12)
The Clere School

What Am I?

My fur is as black as the night's sky,
My eyes are round like the moon.
I am scared of nothing
But scary to everyone.
I hide up trees, as it's the best place to catch my dinner.
I have powerful legs, long and lean
Just like an athlete.
Too strong for most animals,
No need for a home
As I can sleep anywhere.
I can move stealthily and slyly
To catch my dinner.
Thud, and my dinner is ready.
What am I?

Edward Rawlings (12)
The Clere School

What Am I?

My eyes are like big black marbles,
They stare at you all day long.
I am a small fluff ball,
But I would be if I was part of the bear family.
I crawl up trees,
And I eat a certain type of leaf.
My legs are short, stumpy sticks
Which have sharp claws on the end of them.
I live in the rainforest
But soon I will become extinct.

What am I?

Emily Gatehouse (12)
The Clere School

What Am I?

People think I am sly and slimy
But I only want to eat
But I can't stand vegetables
And all I like is meat.

I will sit in the tallest grass,
Many, many hours will pass
But you couldn't find me, even with a spyglass
But I can see you in the sun, I can see you in the moon
And after I strike I can fit you in my mouth
Without a knife, fork or spoon.

But I am as thin as a twig
But as strong as an ox
And I could bite you through a sound-proof box.

What am I? - A snake

Nathan Prince (13)
The Clere School

The Killer Barnacle

Niffer the barnacle was a killer,
It was stuck to the pillar,
Its diamond sharp spikes
And its poisonous spikes
And its poison it strikes
To kill you there and then.

It waits for the not knowing
It kills and keeps growing!
Niffer the barnacle the reddest thing there
It's the only one around anywhere.
So that's why you never go near
A big red barnacle.

Chris Clements (13)
The Clere School

Rabbit

I was just sitting there,
Just sitting under a tree
Then he spotted me.
With his bright red eyes,
Bright as the red sky at night.
Watching my every move,
Every step and every blink.
Then suddenly he started running,
Pounding towards me.
His tongue fell out of his dribbling mouth,
His big buck yellow teeth, almost like fangs,
Stuck out from his face.
He was like a running machine on full power.
I was thinking - *how could something so soft*
And so sweet be so scary?
I got the nearest stick and hit him
Just as he pounced up at me -
And with a big bang
He fell to the floor.

Paige Prior (11)
The Clere School

What Am I?

My fur is white like snow,
I am as hairy as a Wookie.
My teeth are like large white dog claws.
My habitat is a sleepy, slipper, snowy settlement.
Crunch, crunch - as the snow falls from the mountainside
To the ground below.
As loose as a dead moose.
My legs and arms are as long as tree boughs
And my feet are larger than bushes.

What am I?

Ryan Bardoe (12)
The Clere School

The Dying

In the night
The kid watched under her sky of stars
Through the graveyard of misty dreams.
Not able to be
Not able to see.
Her face went as black as a page
As she saw her grave.
The grave of herself
Like some sick dream
Never realising fate
Came too close for comfort
Torturing as this might be
Her dream came true
As it was easy to see.
Misfitting, misfortune
She didn't want to believe
She never wanted time to end
Or her thoughts to leave.

Hannah Read (12)
The Clere School

The Falcon

There I wait for my prey,
I search high and low
And I can see something grey,
So then I strike.
I swoop down
Then grasp it.
It take it to the mountain wall.
Every night I go and search
No one sees
Because I'm black like night.
When the hear me,
They run.

Nathan Cheshire (12)
The Clere School

Have You Ever Wondered?

Have you ever wondered
If there was something out there
And not just the
Stars and the planets.

Have you ever wondered
If there were different people out there
Who drive hovercrafts
And live on Mars.

Have you ever wondered
If there were aliens and spaceships
That go really fast.

Have you ever wondered
If you could visit the aliens
And the people who drive hovercrafts.
Or maybe take a ride in the super fast
Spaceship;
Maybe you will one day
Or you'll just have to look out for those spaceships.

Meg Hatton (13)
The Clere School

The Thing In The Corner

The black thing in the corner
Rubs its wings up against the cage.
It grabs the metal with its old black beak.
Suddenly it topples the cage over
And I see the thick crown on its head.
It swoops towards me and suddenly
There is a massive black scar on its right wing.
It grabs hold of me,
Blood trickles down its mouth.
I phone for an ambulance
But it's too late.

Bradley Smith (13)
The Clere School

You Can't Teach An Old Dog New Tricks

A pity because the tricks they can do
Are absolutely no use to you.
Amazing at obeying when you say 'Stay'
But do they remember your mum's birthday?
Terrific at fetching sticks
Hopeless at writing limericks.
Brilliant at scratching off fleas
But no good at finding lost keys.
The best at stealing your mum's newly-made pies
Useless at choosing suitable ties.
Brilliant at chewing the postman's leg
But a failure at making bacon and egg.
Perfect at coming when you call 'Max'
Not a clue about paying the tax.
Wonderful at licking your face
No idea about picking an ace.
You think he will make a wonderful pet
But have you tried taking him to the vet?
If you're thinking about training your canine pet
It will be best if you just forget.

Victoria Mackenzie (13)
The Clere School

Hamster

He is small, he's agile,
He's very quick
And he will bite you
If you're not quick.
So watch out
When the hamster's about
Or he will bite you with his big fierce teeth
Or scratch you with his razor-sharp nails.
So watch out
When the hamster's about.

Josh Sealey (12)
The Clere School

Meeting Charlie

Every time you see Charlie
You see a golden yellow long-haired, shaggy dog.
Every time you see Charlie
You can see his dark brown chocolate thoughts.
Every time you see Charlie
He desires to be loved all the time.
Every time you see Charlie
He shows you loyalty, love and devotion.
Every time you see Charlie
You are greeted flailing paws
And a madly swinging golden yellow, bushy tail.
Every time you see Charlie
You feel a cold bright pink tongue
And a black wet nose with saliva
Being sprayed in all directions towards you.
When you have experienced this
You have met Charlie.

Joe Woodward (13)
The Clere School

Evil Hamster

In a horror house
Where there's a hamster larking about
As it's quiet as a mouse
Where hamster bodies are as long as stouts.
Suddenly I see
A red-eyed animal
Running at me
Crack as I trip
Bang as I fall
As the hamster gains on me
I scream for help and I die
But did I?

Leo Minter (13)
The Clere School

Dolphin

I'm cold in the black sea as the sun sets upon it.
I notice movement in the corner of my eye.
I look round, a fin protruding from the water -
Makes me stop in my tracks.
Zigzagging through the blackness.
The spike so shark-like.
Then its head comes up.
A strange hole in the top of its head,
The eyes paralyse me,
The eyes as black as the darkest night.
Its devilish grin is wicked.
The mouth opens wide, pointed sharp teeth bared.
Then a horrible squeaking resounds through the air.
It freezes me from the inside.
Mouth closed, it ducks back under.
It's coming towards me again,
Suddenly it jumps out of the water,
Scaring me out of my wits.
It is a dolphin
Fins as sharp as knives.
Skin like thick grey smoke.
The dolphin wags its tail energetically.
The tail so strong, it scares me stiff.
With a splash, it enters the water
Towards me once more,
Closer, closer, closer!

Bryony Brichard (13)
The Clere School

The Evil Parrot

Mum told me to go outside,
Outside to see the parrot.
He was in his huge pen,
His eyes staring back as beady as an owl's.
As I approached,
He was standing taller and taller.
I approached the cage,
At this point he'd gone crazy
Flying around his cage.
I got to the door
Waiting for my destiny.
I walked inside,
As slow as a snail.
He prepared himself,
Then came charging at me.
I had his food in my hand,
I threw it at him.
It did not work.
His wings as big as a branch,
His feathers colourful as a rainbow
Charging at me.
I ran out of the cage,
Shut the door,
Ran inside.
I thought to myself,
I knew that parrot was evil!

Daniel Turner (12)
The Clere School

Why Is This A Poem About Questions?

Why is a question called a question?
I've always wondered that . . .
Why isn't the question called the answer
And the answer called the question?

My world is full of questions,
And all of them have answers,
But answers to these questions,
I may never know.

I think about these questions,
Wonder, 'Which should I ask first?'
But after thinking for a long time,
I just decide to ask them all!

I get answers from my parents,
And answers from my teachers,
But the answers from my friends,
Never seem to make much sense at all!

So every day I think for a while
See which questions I can answer myself,
And the ones I can I will,
But the rest?

Well, they wait in a line,
An ever growing line,
Of questions to be answered,
That never seem to stop!

But one day, I'll look back and see,
That finally, only one question follows me,
But you see this question's a never before asked question.
'Why don't I have any new questions following me?'

Nikki Slater (13)
The Clere School

Feelings

Why can't I be that girl?
The one who you talk to all your friends about?
The one you want to be with?
Why can't I be your girl?

Let's just be 'friends'
The words of the end.
But this broken heart gets worse;
Every single day . . .

Secretly you're the only thing that lifts me up;
And makes me smile.
All the little things that annoyed me;
Are the things I miss so much, now you're gone.

I'm known for being the girl who always smiles;
Even with this torn up heart inside me.
I brighten up people's days;
Yet I can't brighten up my own.

I miss the way you used to look at me;
With those beautiful brown eyes.
The way you'd hold me close,
Never to let me go.
The way you'd kiss my forehead
And the way you'd warm up my heart.
Those three words meant so much.

My mind wants to give up;
But my heart won't let me.
So to sum it all up . . .
I love you and you're my everything;
No matter what.

Charlotte Osborne (13)
The Clere School

Love, The Painful Four-Letter Word

Love is a simple word,
Which comes and goes as it pleases,
I say, love don't come that easy,

When a heart is broken,
There is something inside of you,
That just wants to break free,

When you know it's over,
It's like a bullet through your heart,
It's like your whole life has drifted away,

It happens to everyone,
So don't think that it's you,

Since you have been reading this,
Millions of hearts will have been broken,
All around the world.

Melissa Goodwin (13)
The Clere School

No Words

The sun setting in the sky,
The sea silent as I pass by.
Salt water in the air,
As strangers start to stare.

The chilly breeze moving all in sight,
Light fading, turning to night.
The building here to stay,
No matter what anyone says.

The temperature bitter and bleak
Here I am getting weak
You can cut the atmosphere with a knife
In this cycle - we call life.

Hayleigh Passfield (14)
The Clere School

Please Don't Go

I can hear you shouting through day and night,
I hate the sound, it fills me with rage and fright.
Daddy, all I can hear is you sneer and shout,
And Mummy all you can say is, 'I want you out!'

But don't you think of me, shut up here in my room?
Just thinking about this family and its gloomy doom.
You don't care what I want or what I need
As long as you fulfil you, you and your greed.

I love you Daddy, truly I do
But don't you feel the same, don't you love me too?
Daddy don't leave me, please just don't go.
Daddy I got you a present, even tied it with a bow.

Mummy you can fix this, you can fix anything.
Tell him you want him back, tell him everything.
You can't have had nothing, what did your wedding day mean?
Can't you hear me Mummy, even though I scream?

Is it truly over, do I have to learn to accept?
Is this all there is, nothing else to expect?
Daddy's gone Mummy, open your eyes and see
How can you do this Mummy, how can you do this to me?

Amy McMillan (13)
The Clere School

Doves

The bird I really love
Above all others is the dove.
Doves are pretty, doves are white,
They don't even tend to bite.

Their beauty has no bound,
When they fly there is no sound,
Hence the reason why I love,
Above all other birds, the dove.

Claire Paterson (13)
The Clere School

Hate

Hate is a strong emotion;
One which is opposite to devotion . . .
Firstly you can't judge me;
If you don't even know me . . .
You may know that hate can cause jealousy.
Is this one of the reasons you hate me?
It's funny how you used to be my mate;
Now all you have is hate . . .
If you hate me, then obviously
You don't know the real me . . .
But then again;
What you see is what you get . . .
You can't hate me because . . .
You'll never be me!

Simone Such (14)
The Clere School

My Magical Place

The sunlight dazzles you, shining in every empty space.
The appreciation and affection reflected by the smiles on our faces.
When it comes to midday, the lions are purring away
Just like happy cats.

The hippos and elephants gulping down streams of water
As if their lives depended on it.

Magical birds surrounding the canopies of the trees.
Searching for every last juicy orange in sight.
The birds see the chickens in a pen just waiting for food.
Wow! The magical colours. This is a once in a lifetime opportunity.

My brothers, my sisters and myself are having the time of our lives
Surrounding every oak tree and every meadow in sight.

Wow what a magical place to be, especially on a day like this.
I get to share it with my family, that makes it so much better.

Abi Golding (13)
The Clere School

A Year . . .

A year of hugging
A year of laughing
A year of cute text messages
A year with the person I love.

A year of kissing
A year of loving
A year of holding hands
With the person I love.

A year of your warmth
A year of your love
A year of our love
A year of true love.

One year with you
Is a century of paradise
Is a year of happiness
A year unforgettable, passionate
A year with you,
That's all I want.

Claire Purser (13)
The Clere School

Mystery

I am swimming alone
The sea is as blue as the sky.

A small orange dot catches my eye,
It looks at me and then moves towards me
Sending shivers down my spine.

As it comes closer, it gets clearer,
It has small scratches on both its sides.
It starts to open its mouth
When suddenly . . .

JJ Paine (14)
The Clere School

Into The Blue

No one knows what's out there
No one's seen it all
There's no map to guide you
Into the blue.

A vast expanse of nothingness
A bus ride to nowhere
The place of pure calm
Into the blue.

The biggest hiding place ever
The spirit of the world
A mix of many emotions
Into the blue.

No one knows what's out there
No one's seen it all
There is no map to guide you
Into the blue.

Lara Eaton (13)
The Clere School

Fairies

Far, far away
In a fairy-tale land,
Pixies and fairies
All hold hands.

At the end of the garden
In a mushroom ring,
All of them shout,
Dance and sing.

And when it is night
They all fly away
And sleep until
Another day.

Fran Duggan (13)
The Clere School

Australia

The warmth, the heat, the gorgeous sun,
The wallabies the wombats,
The kangaroos, the dingoes.
Why would anyone want to leave?

The easy life, the relaxation,
The amazing holiday views,
The barbecues and outdoor eating,
Who would want to go and see?

The sea, the beaches, the massive waves,
The twenty-four hour surfing,
The Great Barrier Reef and the great ocean road,
Why don't you go and see for yourself.

Jenny Harris (13)
The Clere School

Dance

I listen to the music playing
My soul swings to its beat.
As the melody and rhythm
Descend to my feet.

I dance to the music playing
My heart beats in tune
As I breathe with the rhythm
I let out a sigh.

My body becomes tuned
As I wrap up the song
I rehearse for hour
Now it's time to finish . . .

Hannah Jones (13)
The Clere School

Last Breath, Dying Thoughts

Long lost words whisper slowly to me,
Still can't find what keeps me here inside.
I lie here
And I'm pouring crimson regret and betrayal.
My headstone's engraved with the tools of my mind
And my grave's already been dug.
The skeletons of my past will be buried beside me
Fifty feet in the mud.
My breath rises in short, sharp breaths
And clogs the air around me.
I choke and stutter as my throat heaves,
As memories flash black and white
Through my mind.
One stands out
Much too vividly,
I force it out but it pushes back.
A trusted friend,
A steely glint,
A short, sharp shock, then
Silence.
And now I lie here
And I'm pouring crimson regret and betrayal.

Charlotte Jones (13)
The Clere School

Emptiness

All alone in an empty room,
A tear trickled down his dry coarse face.
Clenching his head in his hands,
His crumbled heart, it will never be mended.

In the dusk-covered area he sat
Alone in the freezing apartment in the depths
Of the night,
The woman he loved was . . . dead!

The despondent man was suicidal,
His life was unbearable.
Grasping a hold of her last possession
He got up.

He put his last shot of energy,
Into shuffling towards the mysterious window
He cried his last emotional tear
He looked at the sky for the very last time.

I will love you forever my girl,
I'm coming darling.
H had spoken his last words
As he raised the jet black object to his head.

Claire Pastemakiewicz (14)
The Clere School

Alcohol!

When people think of alcohol, they think it's just a drink,
It livens up a party and alters the way you think.
It makes you feel more confident to let yourself go wild,
It's not going to kill you the effects of it are mild.

When I think of what people think, I think those thought aren't true,
If more people saw the effect it has, would they think the way I do.
I knew someone who liked his drink, he binged throughout the year,
From binging to obsession, he couldn't cope without his beer.

When informed he had a problem, he was in complete denial
He carried on drinking, but only for a while.
Admitted into hospital, he was going to die,
With just two days left, I asked the question why?

His organs were failing, one per cent of his liver left,
Taking his life away from me was alcohol committing theft.
So next time you look at alcohol remember the effects and think
Is it really worth it. Think before you drink.

Chelsea Johnson (15)
The Garth Hill School

I Need You Back - I'm Homeless

I'm ashamed,
I'm homeless.
This is very pointless
What would you do
If this situation was left to you?

I haven't got a home
And I have no friends.
People take the mick
It makes me very sick.
Shall this just be the end.

People pass me by
Through the streets they fly.
I'm wandering how long it will be
Until someone comes to rescue me.

So please, please, please
Come and get me.
I need you more now than I can ever say
And when I get back I'll be with you this way.

Carrie Taylor (14)
The Willink School

The Horrid Teacher

A war is going on in school,
It has turned uncool.
The winded rhino charges on.
Can this be true? Is it a con?
One whole year in this old place,
Stuck in here, looking at her ugly face.

Her eyes are black spots,
Gazing all around.
Her hair is a brown lump,
Stuck in a mound.
Her lips open really wide,
Wide as a football.
She makes a deafening sound.
She makes a horrific call.
Will we win this deadly war?
Quick, hide!
She's coming down the corridor.
Yikes!

She used to be a horrible witch.
What a change, what a switch.
This grumpy hag,
Who smells like mouldy fags,
Has transformed into nice,
Sweet, sugar and spice.

She's talking about a boyfriend,
The one she never had.
Apparently he makes her happy,
That's why she's no longer sad.

Her mound of thick hair
Now swirls behind her head.
Her attitude has changed too,
'Good morning,' she said.
This strange woman,
This mindless bat.
I hope they'll be happy,
Miss Lollyope and Mr Matt.

Rebecca Hill (14)
The Willink School

Why Did Love Have To Die?

Sorry but I have to say,
That the person I loved has just passed away.
His spirit came out and flew up to the sky.
Why did he have to die?

He's watching down on me,
From high above
I need a key
The key that opens the door into Heaven.

I want him to come home,
Because in this life I'm all alone.
Sad and crying and thinking of you
I want you back,
So you can make me happy again.

Rebecca Howarth (13)
The Willink School

The Bomb

Loudly the bomb went off,
Loudly the scream came from the town,
Loudly I cried when I saw the cloud,
Loudly my feet pounded the ground as I ran.

Nervously I walked through the town,
Nervously I saw all the dead bodies,
Nervously I walked towards our shop,
I jumped as my dad came round the corner.

Quietly he spoke to me,
Quietly I went and sat,
Quietly I cried when I heard Mum was dead,
Quiet the town was after the bomb.

Gareth Scott (13)
The Willink School

£1,000

Oh what I could do
with £1,000
I could buy a TV
and have surround sound.
I'd find an old car
nearly falling apart
and make it real nice
with fantastic new parts.
If I needed more clothes
I'd have a shopping spree
and buy gorgeous new dresses
entirely for me.
I'd go on a trip
that's exotic and hot
and take all my friends,
amazing, or what?
Oh the things I could do
it would be so cool.
Oh no hang on a minute
the money's gone to my school

Rachel Winter (14)
The Willink School

Young Writers Information

We hope you have enjoyed reading this book - and that you will continue to enjoy it in the coming years.

If you like reading and writing poetry drop us a line, or give us a call, and we'll send you a free information pack.

Alternatively if you would like to order further copies of this book or any of our other titles, then please give us a call or log onto our website at www.youngwriters.co.uk

**Young Writers Information
Remus House
Coltsfoot Drive
Peterborough
PE2 9JX**

(01733) 890066